CRICUT EXPLORE AIR 2

UNPACK YOUR SKILLS!
TIPS AND TRICKS FOR THE MASTER USE OF
YOUR CRICUT EXPLORE

Made with love

by

Sienna

Tally

Table of Contents

Introduction

To simply put: The Cricut Explore Air 2 is an electronic cutting machine. It bears a resemblance to your typical printer; however, this device doesn't print out your design paper. Instead, it cut out almost anything you can imagine. Whether it is decals, vinyl labels, paper crafts, shirts, fabrics, etc., it is no problem for the Cricut. It can achieve this due to the series of rollers and very accurate blades specially designed for it.

Cricut has a series of machines that perform this function, such as the Cricut Expression and the Gypsy, but the Cricut Explore Air 2 stands out from all others. Cricut Explore Air 2 is mostly due to its updated design library inventory system. Unlike other machines that use cartridges, the Explore Air is allowed access to Cricut Access and their massive library of cut files. You may upload and cut your files. You could also make use of the user-friendly software on your tablet or computer, with or without an internet connection. It not only cuts over 100 different materials, but it also allows you to write, score, and draw with it.
You will undoubtedly be amazed and stunned by the top-notch engineering of the machine.

It is also pretty easy to use. The simplest tasks merely make use of the Design Space to design whatever you intend to cut. Then you fit your material on the cutting mat, calibrate your settings, and start cutting.
There is hardly any limit to the uses of a Cricut Explore machine.

So, if you're just filled with tons of DIY, crafts, or party ideas, then the Cricut Explore Air 2 is the machine for you!

How Much Can the Cricut Explore Air 2 Do?

Whatever you need to cut out, etched, drawn, or score, the Cricut is the machine for the job. Below is a brief list of projects ideas for your Cricut:

- Rather earrings
- Paper gift boxes
- Vinyl quotes for teacups
- Greeting cards
- Monogrammed water bottles
- Vinyl labels for pantries
- Decals for model airplanes
- Iron-On Vinyl t-shirts
- Stencils for wood signs
- Felt coasters
- Customized tote bags
- Paper flowers
- Coloring books

And many more.

Where You Can Buy the Cricut Explore Air 2

This device is all the rage now, and the supply more than matches the demand, so it shouldn't be so hard to find one. However, you have to make sure it's original. With a device like this, you know there are bound to be counterfeited. Below is a list of retails that are sure to have it, affordably and without risk of buying a fake:

- Cricut.com
- Cricut Explore on Amazon
- Michaels
- Target
- JOANN
- HSN

There's no doubt you're already hooked on this device, but perhaps you still harbor doubts about purchasing one. Well, this book will do more than ridding you have that doubt. This book covers the potential benefits of owning a Cricut Explore Air 2. It also does an excellent job of holding your hand as a first-time Cricut user.

Chapter 1
What Is A Cricut Explore Air 2 Machine

This is the youngest sibling of the Cricut Explore line. It is the best of the machines in this line. Explore Air 2 is as efficient as the other ones, but it does its work even better. It even has a better design, and it comes in different colors than you can do.

Capability

The model features a Fast mode that speeds up the cutting process, primarily if you work with deadlines.
It also has the features in the other systems like the German carbide premium blade, inbuilt Bluetooth adapter, dual carriage, and auto-settings.
The great thing about Explore Air is that it is ideal for both beginners and advanced users.

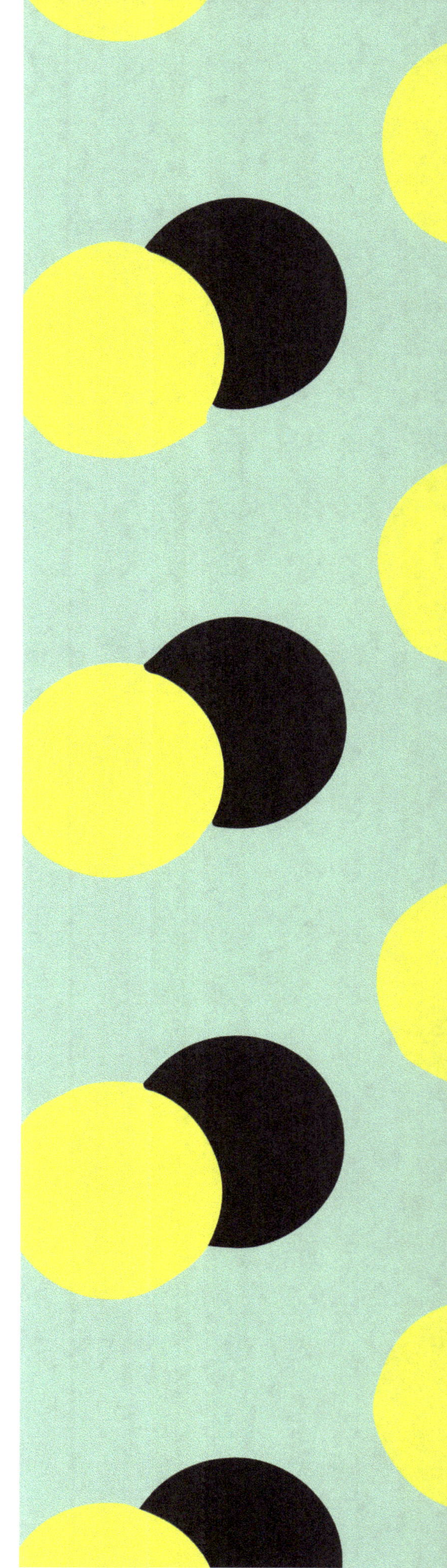

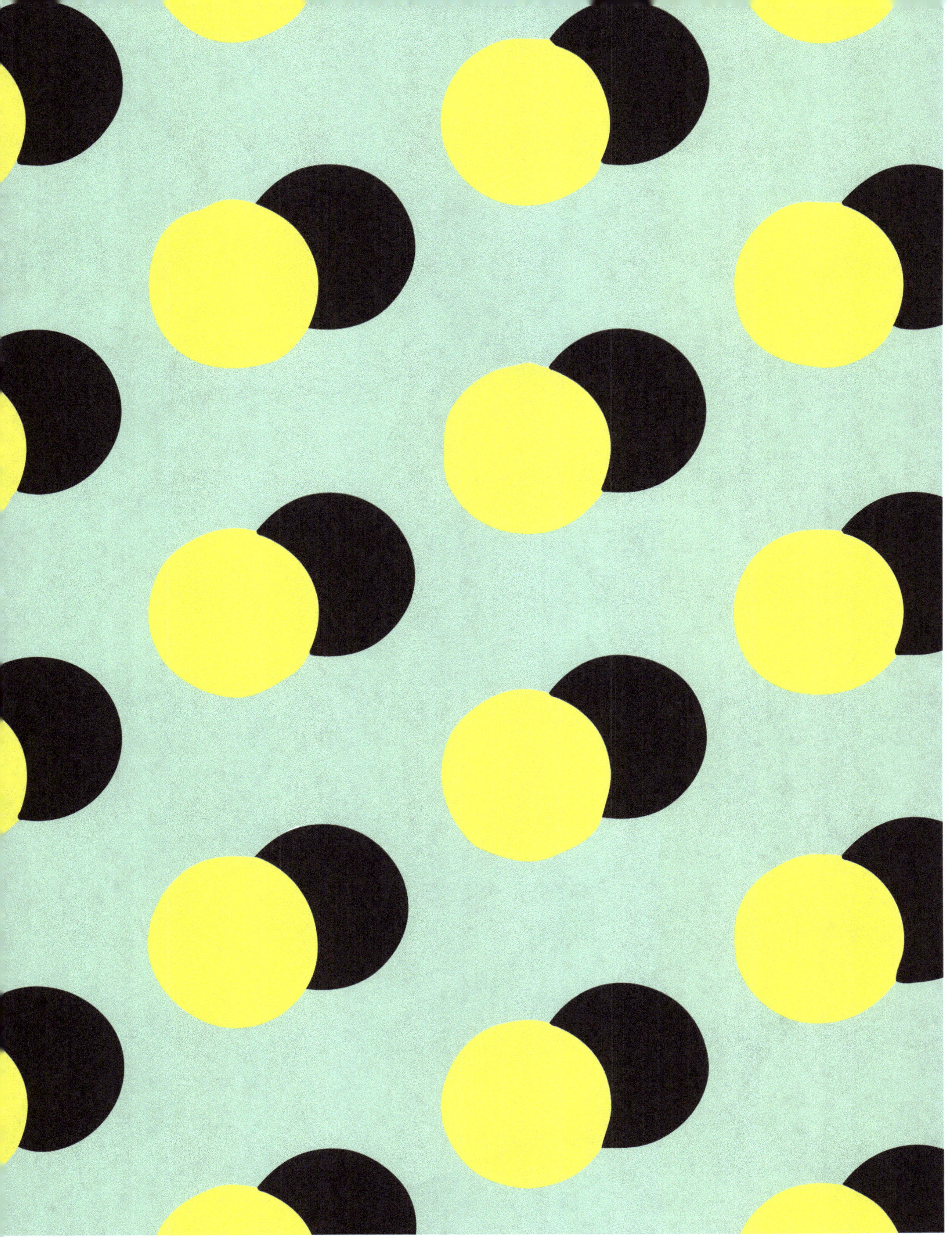

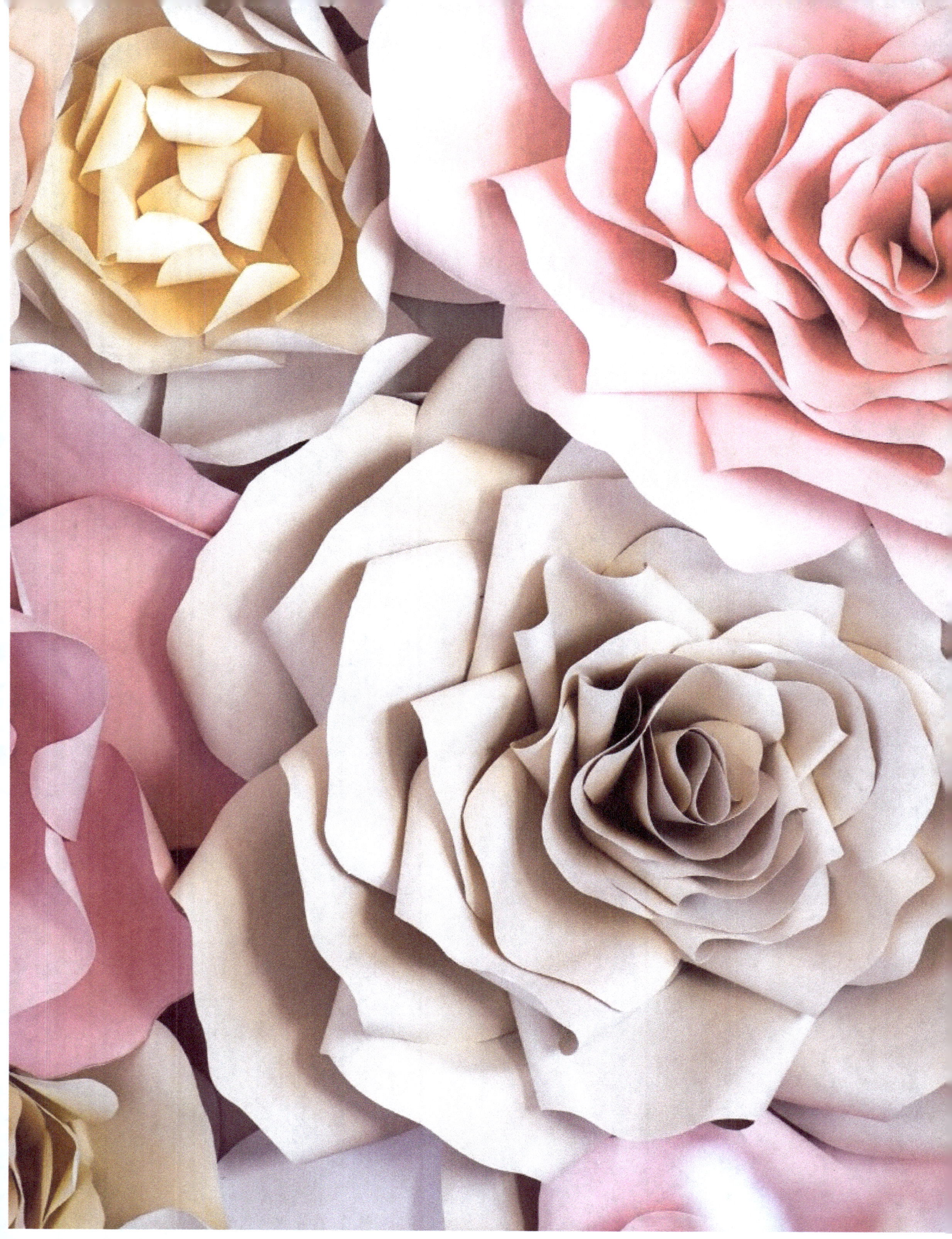

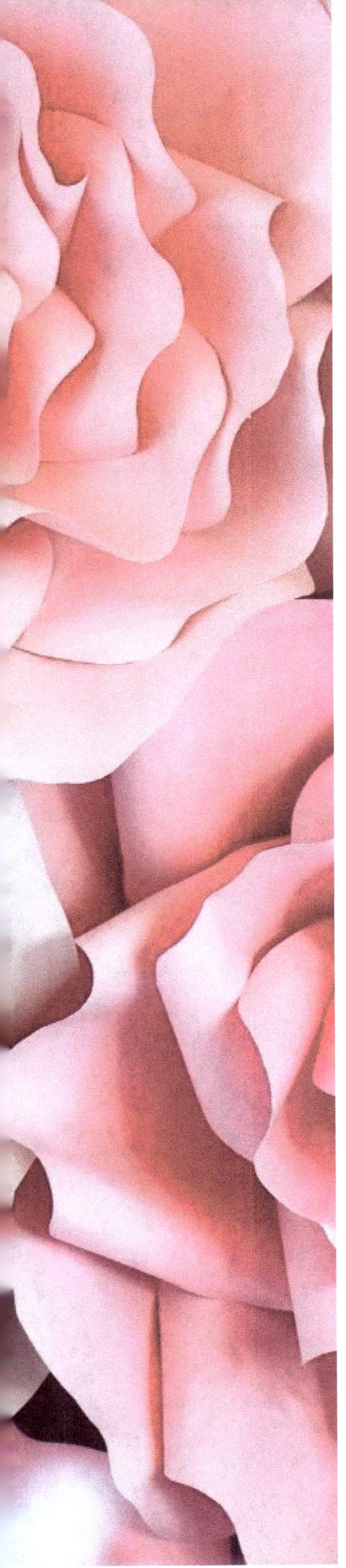

Materials

This machine can cut through a hundred materials or even more. It Is not limited to cotton, silk, tissue paper, corkboard, foil, foam, aluminum, leather, clay, chipboard, burlap, and even birch wood.

It also has the Smart Dial, which helps you manage the cutting width depending on the materials.

Cutting Force

The model is highly potent, and it makes use of the German carbide premium fine point blade, which comes with precision and speed. It is also able to cut any material with a width of 11.5 x 23.5 inches.

When you first purchase a Cricut Explore Air 2, you get a three-month free subscription with access to premium features offered by Cricut! The Cricut Design Space is also cloud-oased for those using iOS devices. With this, you can work offline!

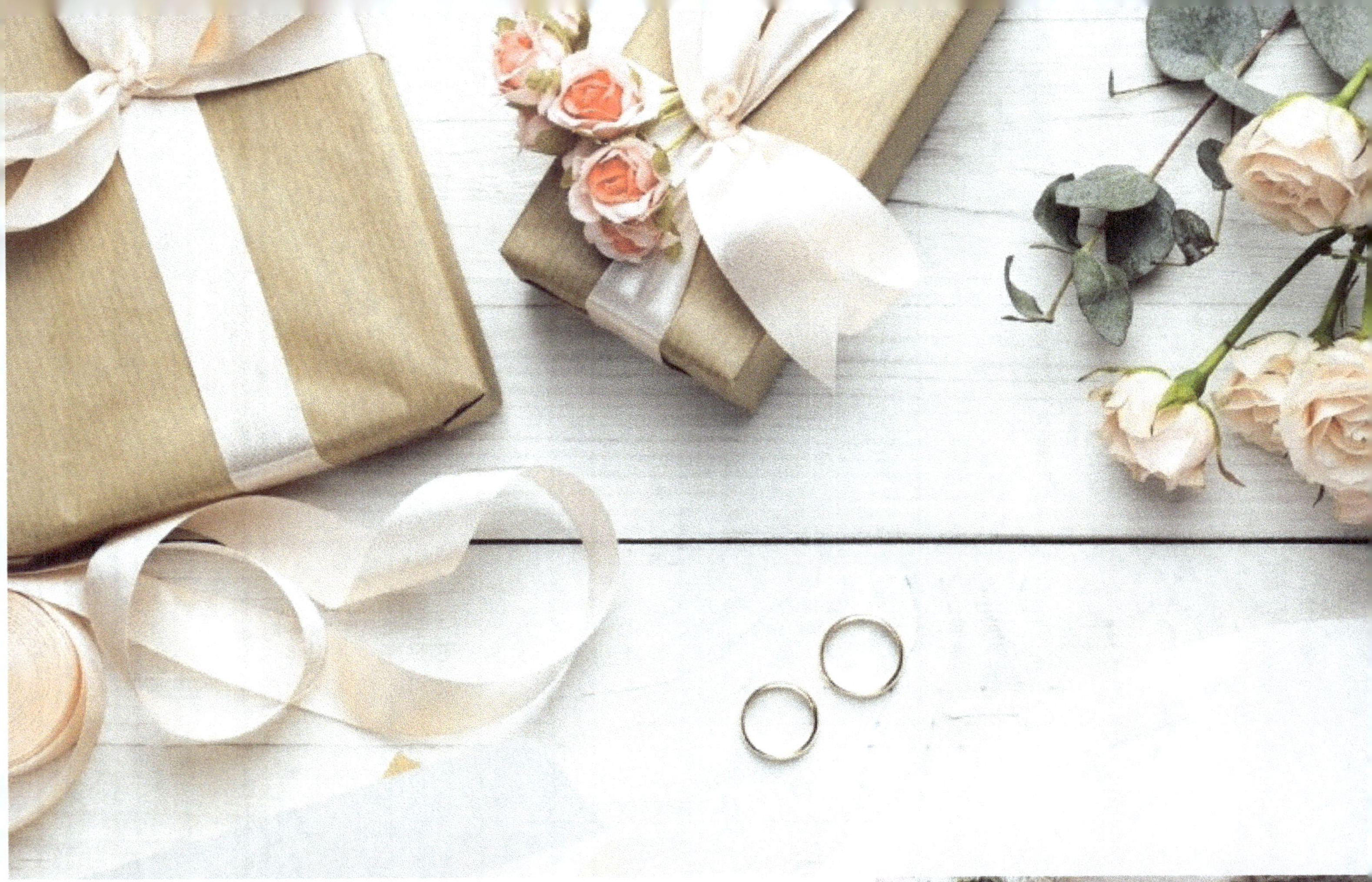

Chapter 2
Unboxing Your Cricut Explore Air 2 And Setting Up

Cricut Explore Air 2 has a unique design. It has a manual intelligent control panel for choosing some pre-defined materials because they are the most used in general.

Thus, your work will be more agile, and you will save time in production. You can choose which material you want to cut just by turning the knob. You can still select the cut level,

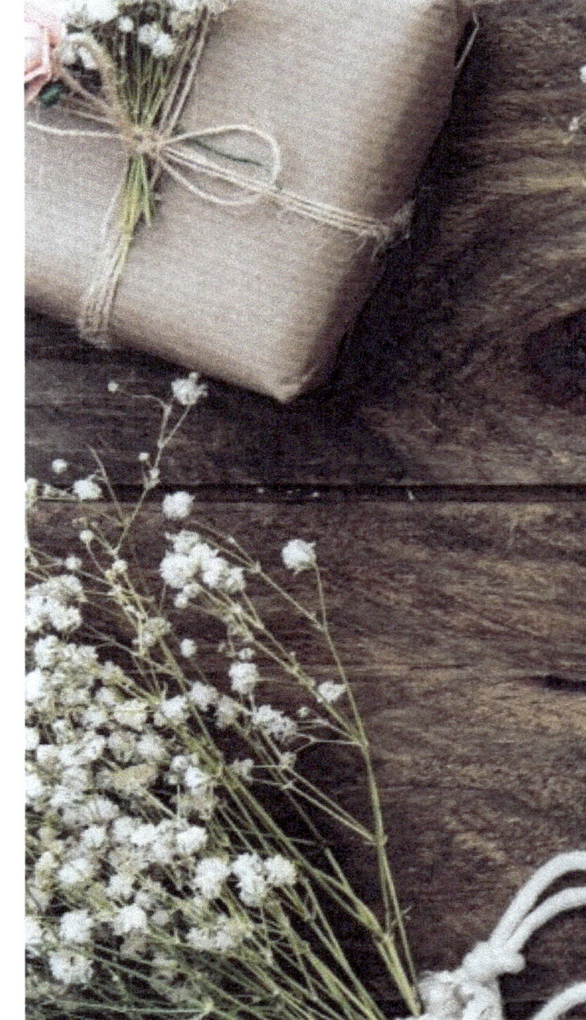

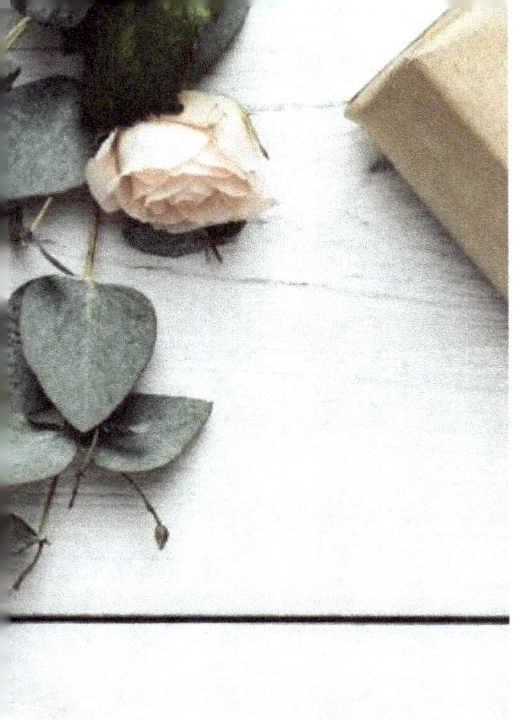

whether you like it weaker or a little more substantial than the standard.

Physical characteristics:
- Height: 14 cm
- Length: 53 cm
- Width: 14 cm
- Weight: approximately 6.7 kg

What's in the box?
- Cricut Explore Air 2 Machine
- Power cable
- USB cable
- 01 Fine Point Blade and its support pre-installed
- 01 Standard (StandardGrip) or Light Fixa-

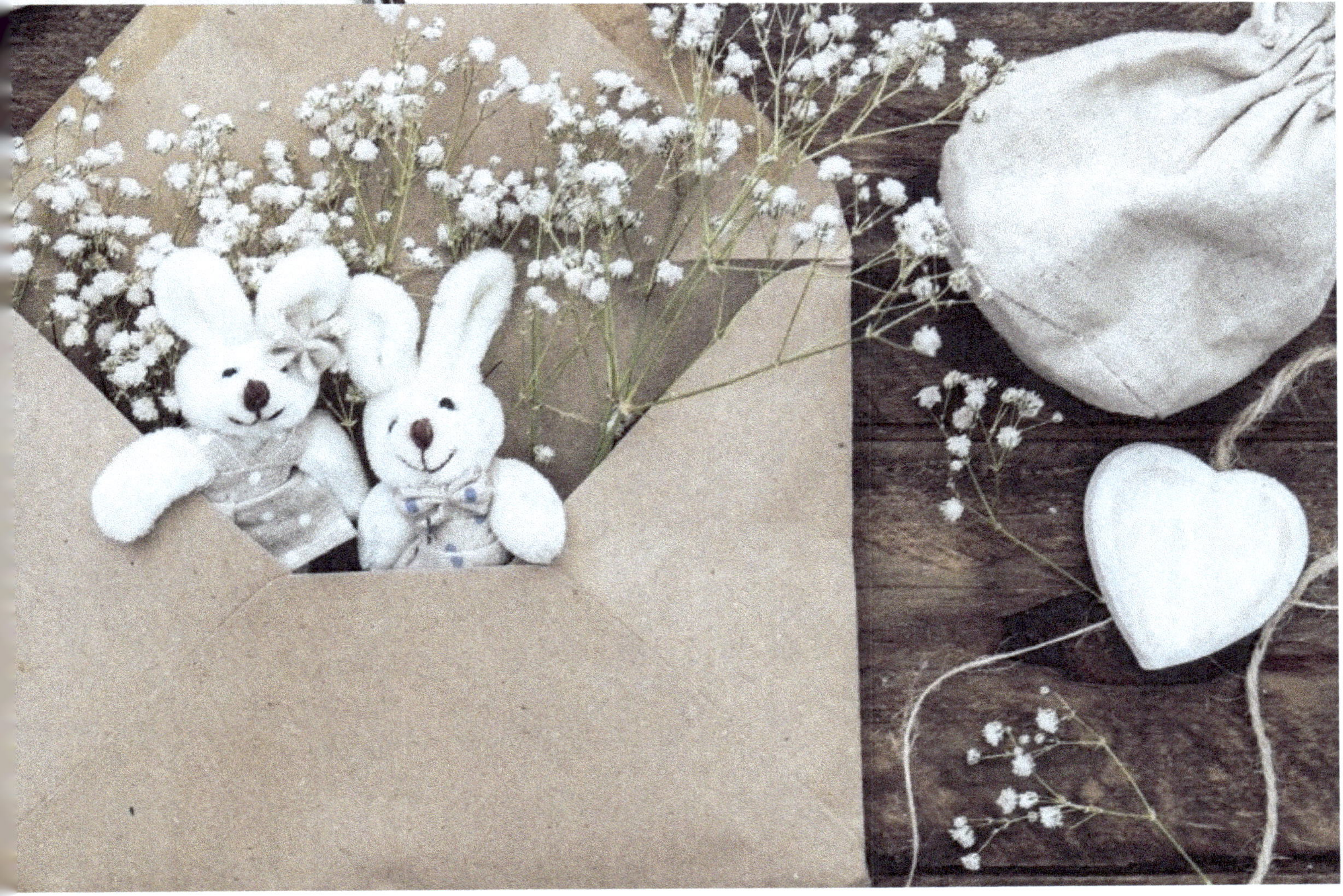

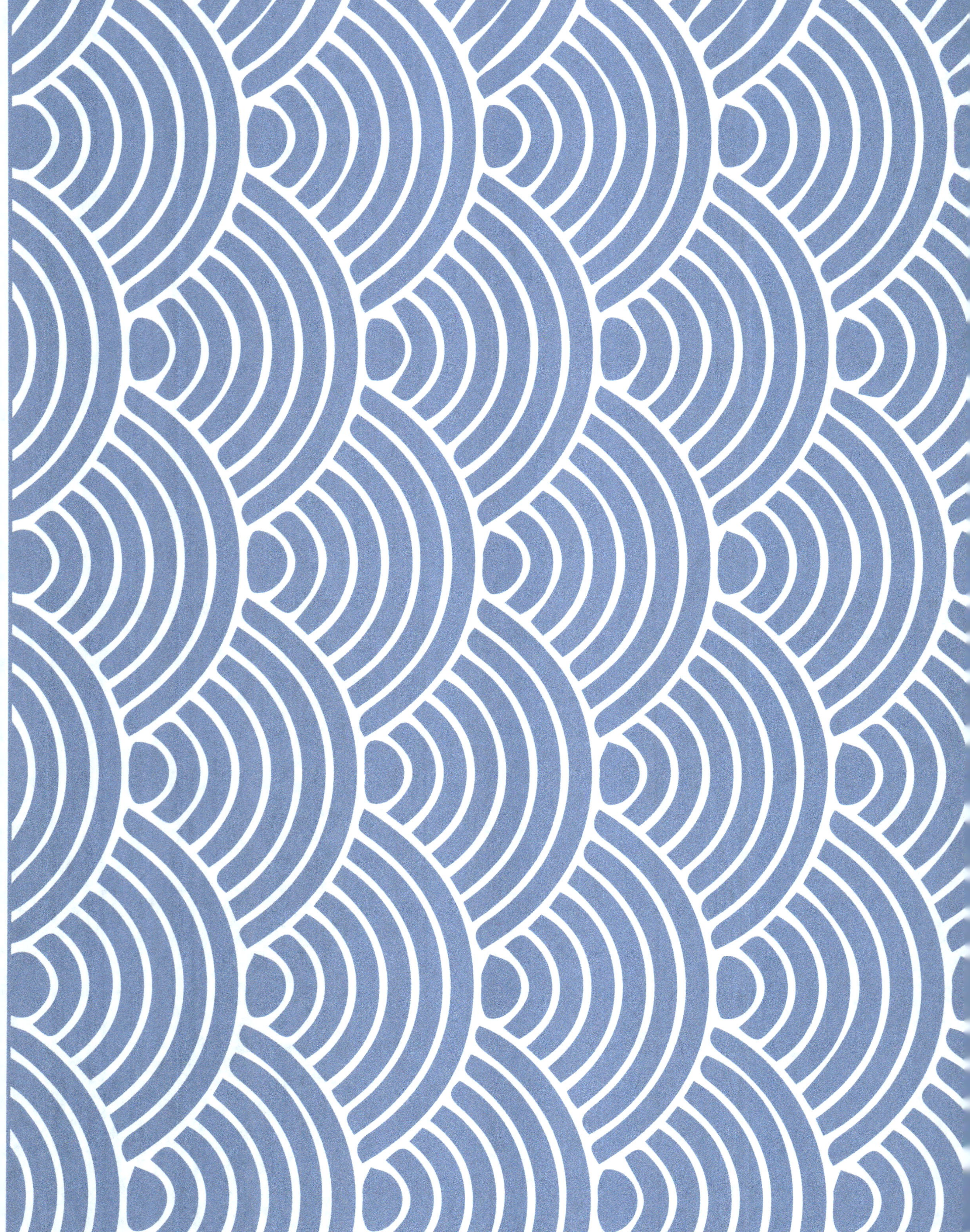

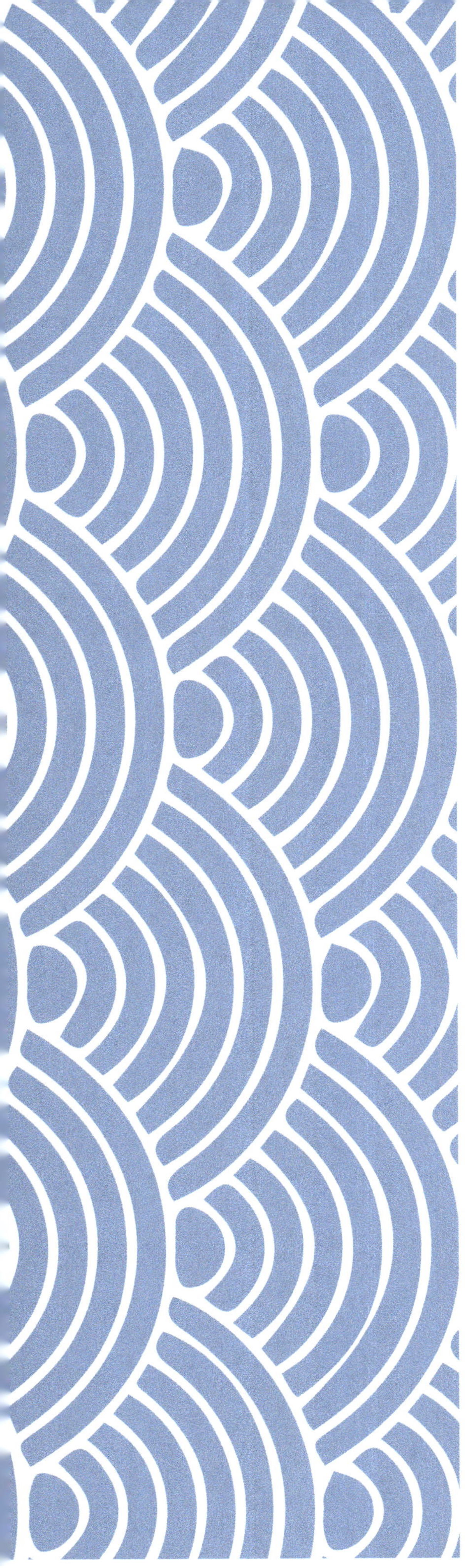

tion (LightGrip) cutting base 30.5 cm x 30.5 cm (12 in x 12 in)

·   Welcome Book

·   Materials for the first project

·   01 Fine tip pen in black color

·   The software provides you with 50 ready-to-use projects

You bought your Cricut Explore Air 2. That incredible machine arrived at your home, but what now? How to install the device and get it ready for use?

How to Install Cricut Explore Air 2

First step: Take your Cricut Explore Air 2 out of the box and check out all its components:

·   Power cable

·   USB cable

·   01 Premium Blade and Thin Tip Blade Holder already pre-installed

·   01 Standard (Standard Grip) or Light Fixation (Light Grip) cutting base 30.5 cm x 30.5 cm (12 in x 12 in)

·   Welcome Book

·   Materials for the first project

·   01 Fine tip pen in black color

·   The software provides you with 50 ready-to-use projects

Items checked successfully, and now it's time to choose where your machine will be. So, here's the tip: to use it, remember to place it in space enough to leave 25cm in front and 25cm behind.

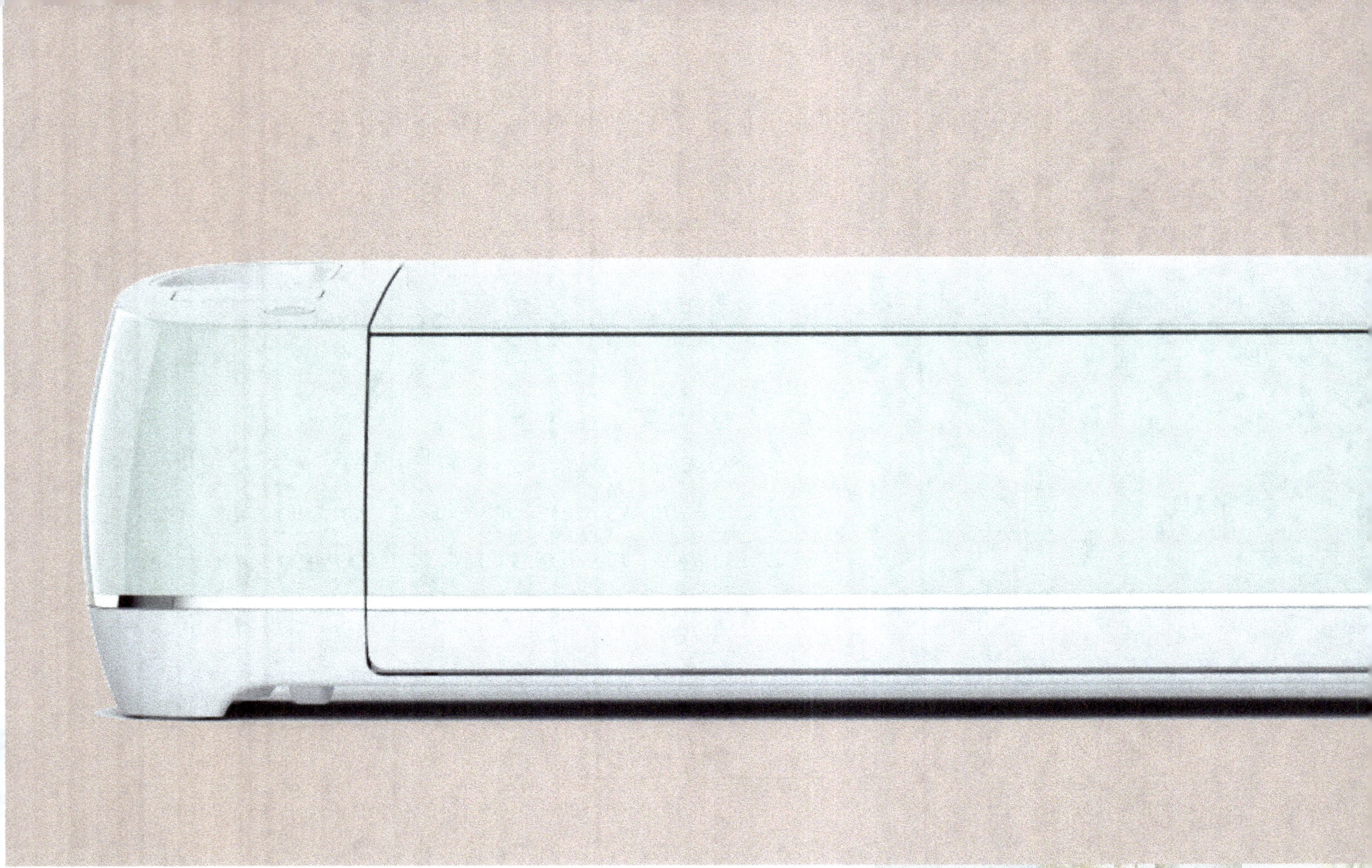

So now press the "OPEN" button...

Wow!

Like magic, an automatic opening is present in front of you! You can take the bucket because you drooled too much! I was also amazed when I opened mine.

Now with great care, remove the seals and protections from all the parts you find.

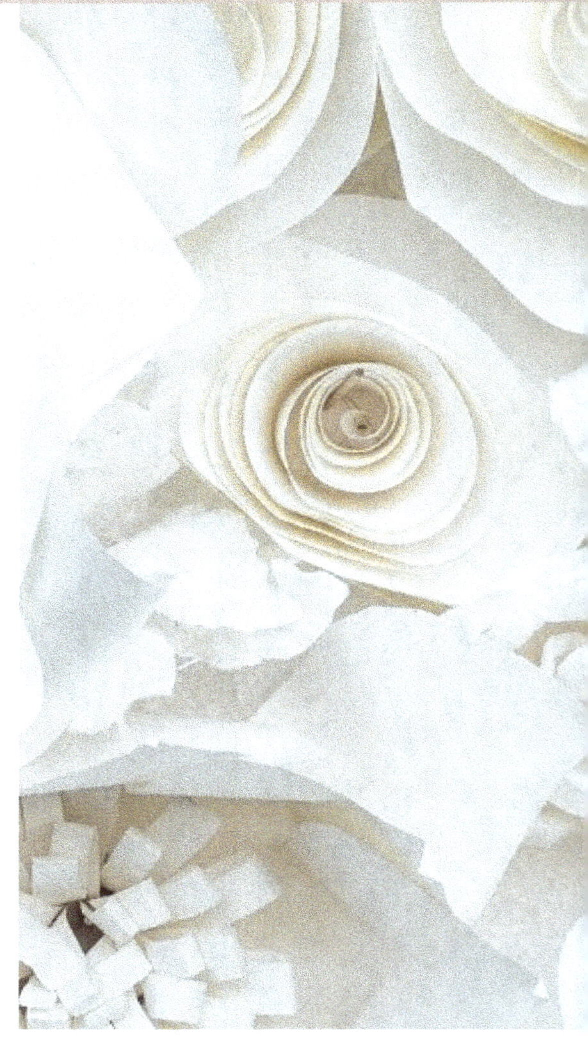

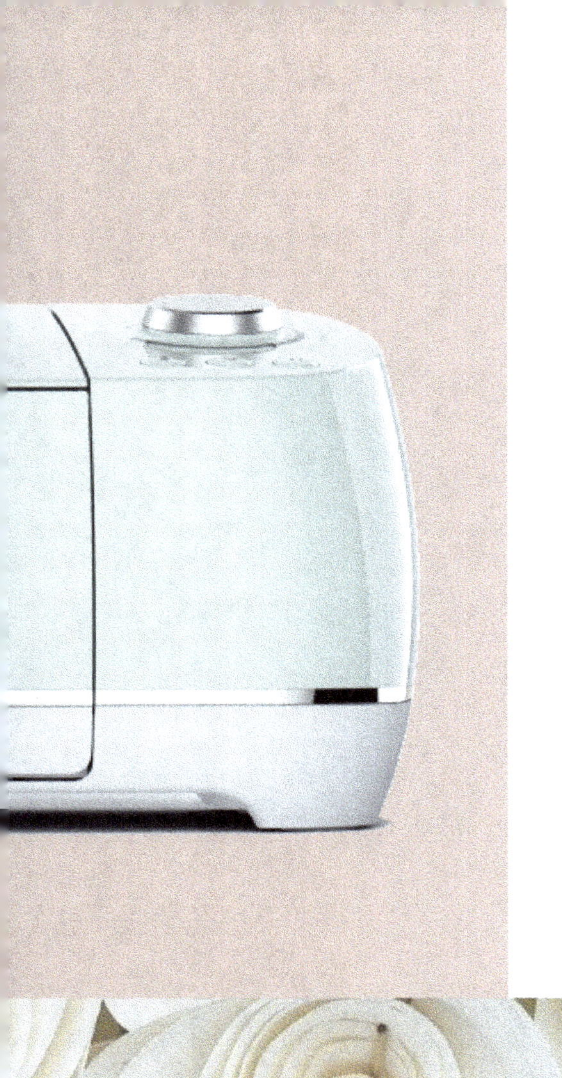

Now, to know a little more about your Cricut Explore Air 2, notice that it has an Intelligent Panel on the right side, which already contains the cutting settings for the most used materials in daily life. However, it cuts out more than 100 fabrics. Yet, we will talk about that later.

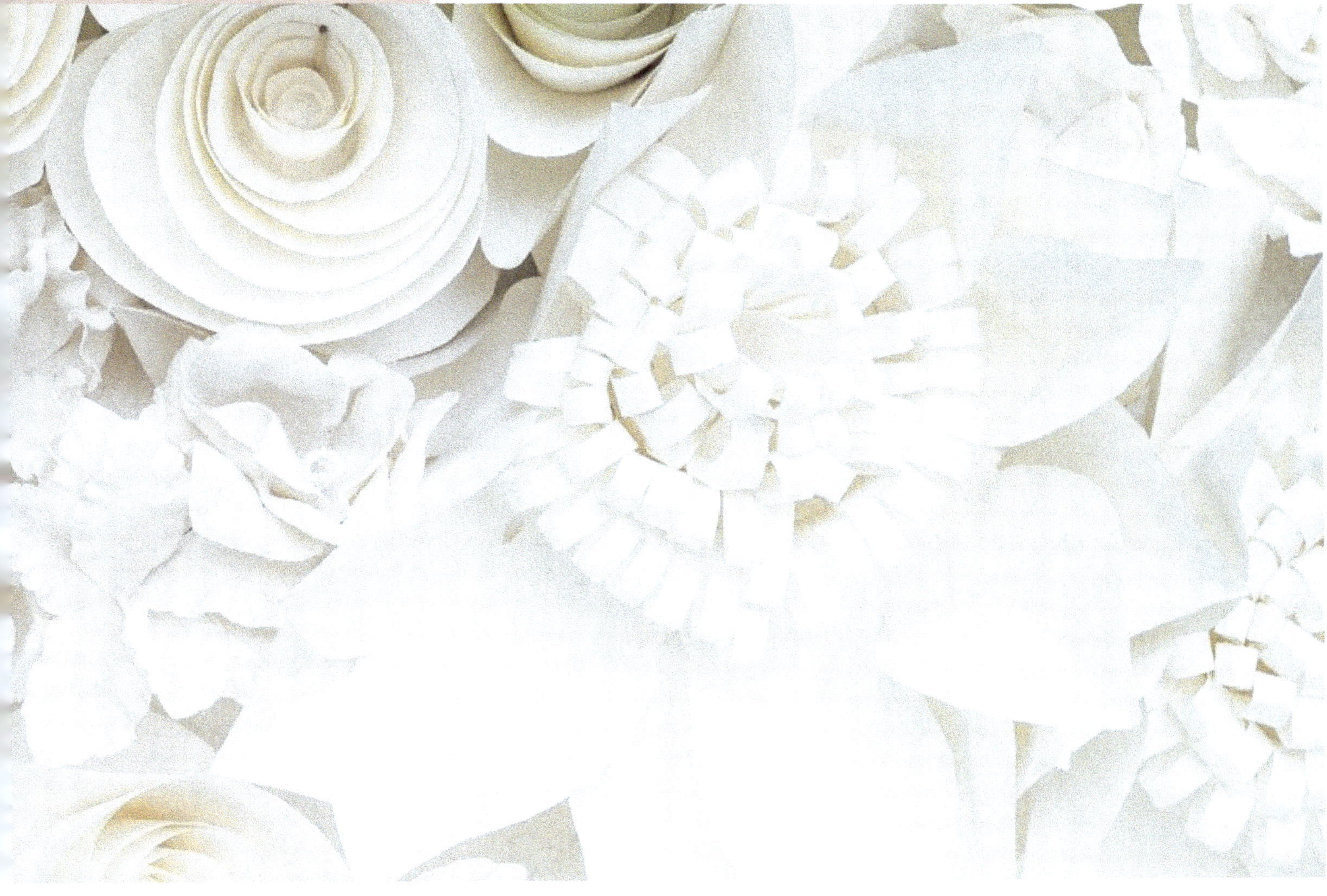

In the central part, there are two "drawers" to store blades and tools. Also, on the left side, there is a compartment for tools and pens. Finally, there is an entry to connect physical cartridges used by people who bought files in this mode in older versions of Cricut machines. Now that they are appropriately presented, let's start by installing the Design Space, following the steps below.

How to Install Cricut Design Space

· Access Design Space in your browser.
· Select the Product you want to configure / Register.
· Design Space is available for Android and iOS, in addition to Windows and iMac. For cellular systems, there is an offline version of the program. However, the offline version is still beta on the computer, so it is not available to all users.
· The next screen prompts you to log in with your Cricut account. If you don't already have a Cricut ID, just create it on this screen. However, if you already have a Cricut ID, just click on the "Login" button and enter your login and password.
· After logging in, click on "Download."

It's time to plug in your Explore Air 2 and turn it on. If you prefer, you can also connect it via Bluetooth since it is already integrated with Cricut Explore Air 2; however, if you need help pairing your computer to Cricut Explore Air 2 via Bluetooth. It can be done at any time so that we can proceed with the connection

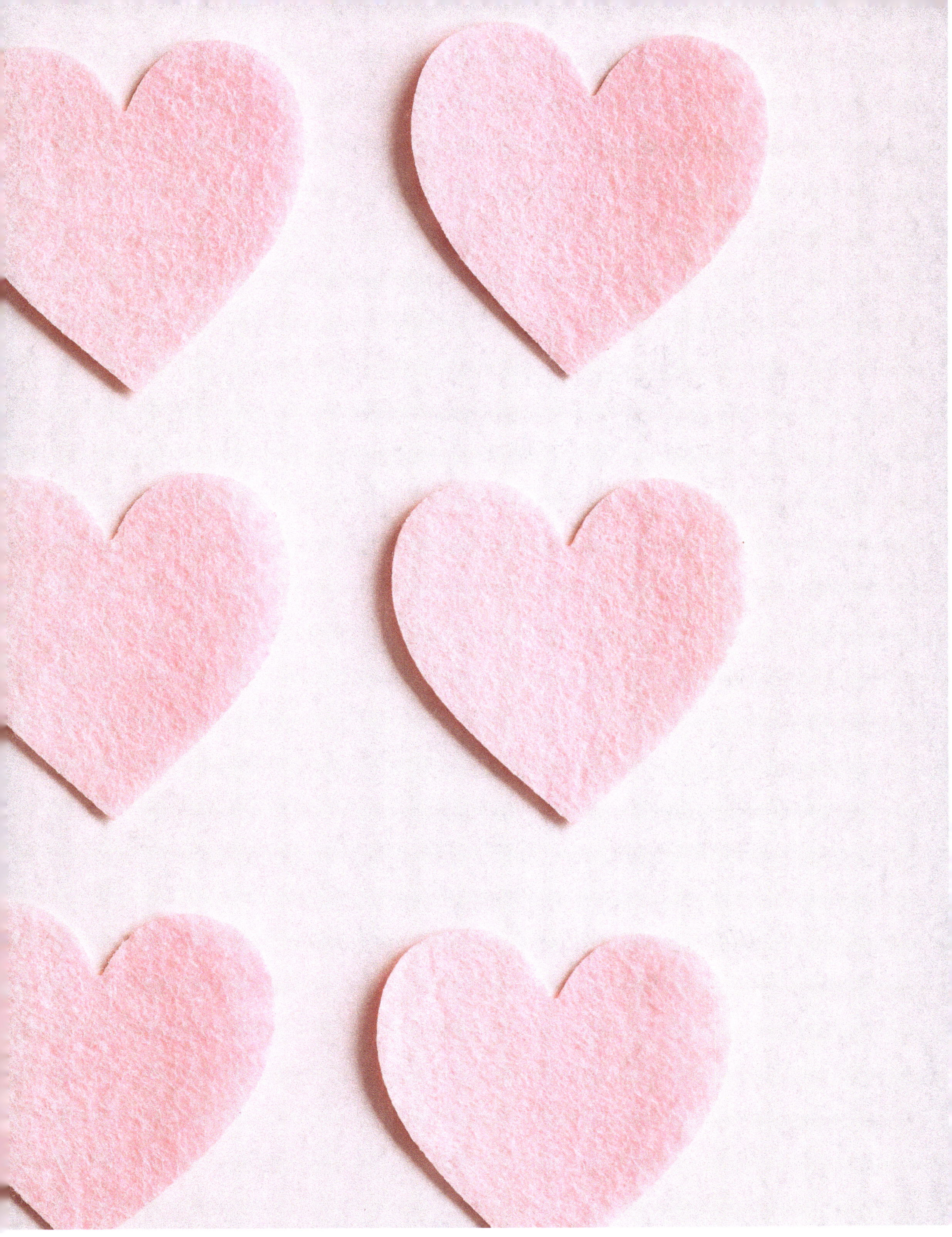

via USB cable. With the machine turned on, the installation process itself checks whether the firmware is up to date or not.

After verification, the next screen shows you the option to subscribe to Cricut Access or not. This is the Cricut store, where you can find thousands of image files, projects, fonts, and many beautiful creations. You can have a free month to try and then cancel your subscription at any time, or you can choose to sub-scribe later. However, if you decide not to sign at this time, don't worry! There are many free designs available for you to use. Well, going back to our subject, the next screen is where it all starts, and you can follow step by step all the commands in detail. Therefore, use the materials and tools that come with the machine: papers, Cricut black pen, and the blade.

Cutting Base, Cutting Blades and Accessories

Now let's talk a little bit about cutting ba-

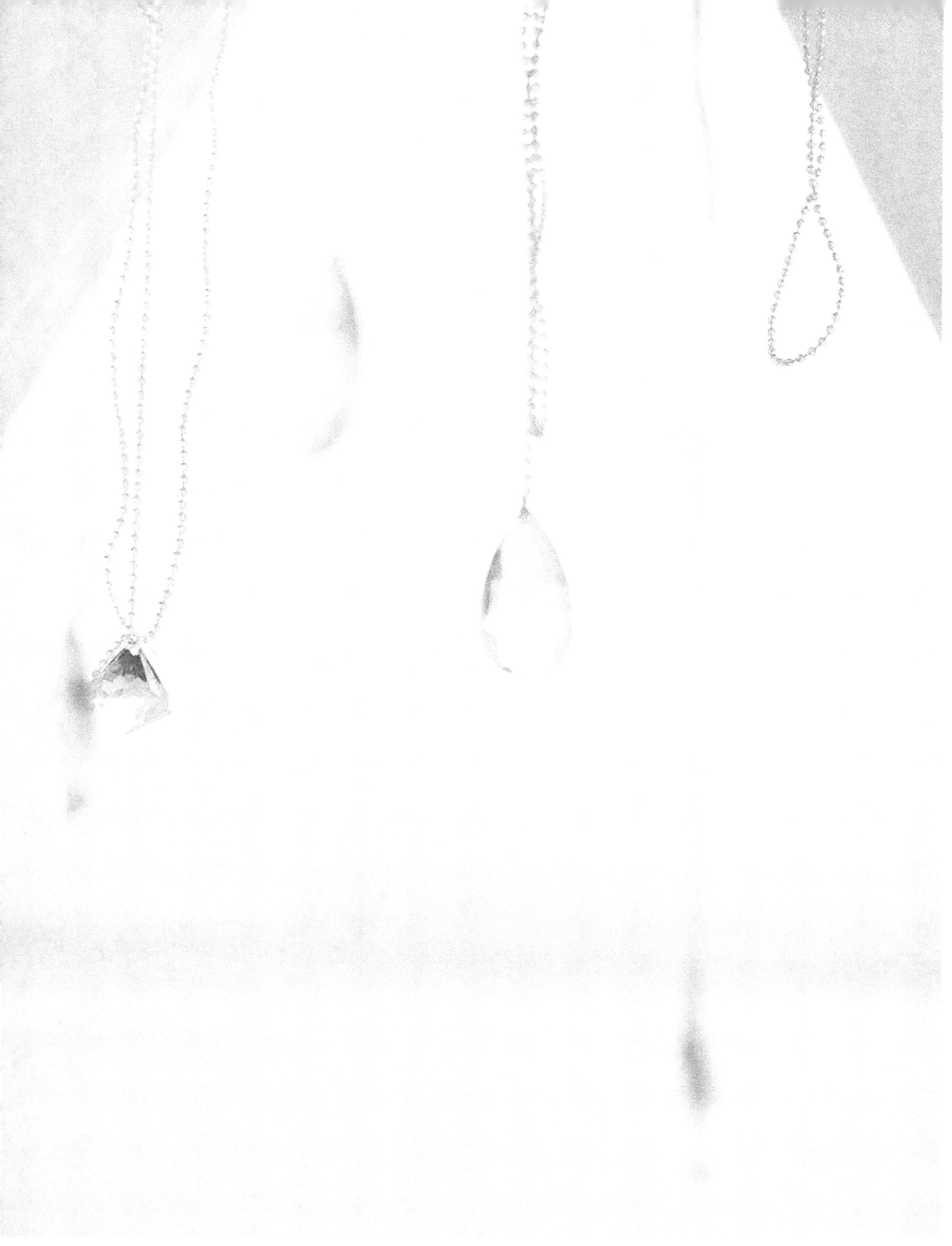

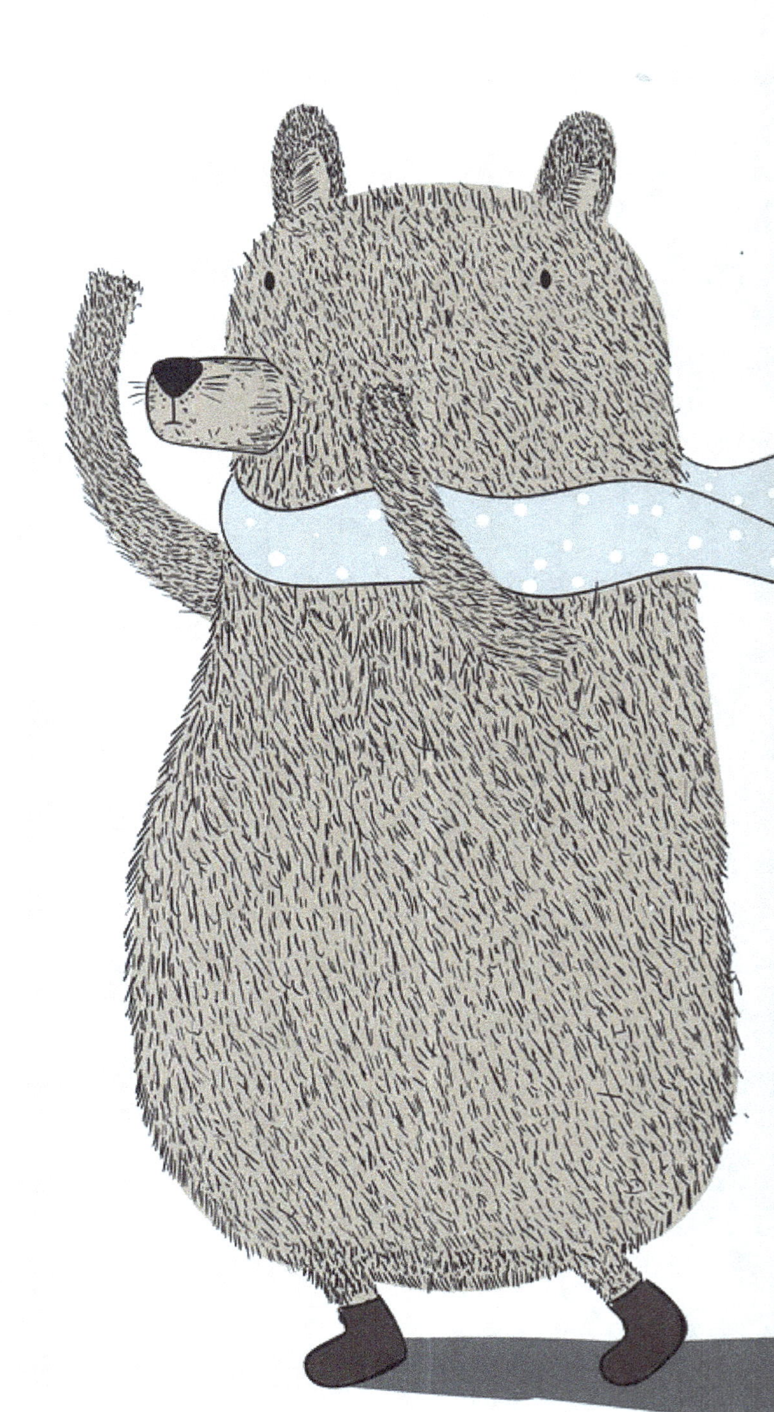

ses, blades, and other accessories that you can use on your Cricut Explore Air 2, in addition to showing some creative possibilities.

CUTTING BASES

There are four types of cutting bases, and all of them can be used in Cricut Explore Air 2. Therefore, for purging, each floor has a color to differentiate the glue's adhesion from each one.

They are:

1. Blue base = light fixation
2. Green base = standard fixation
3. Pink base = specific for fabrics
4. Purple base = for heavier materials.

Important:

The Purple Base is not required for use with Cricut Explore Air 2 because it is more targeted at materials of more excellent thickness cut in the Cricut Maker, but if you want to use it, no problem.

Cricut Cutting Blades

With four types to choose from, the blades that can be used on the Cricut Explore Air 2 are:

For materials up to 1.1mm:

Fine Point Blade (silver) is ideal for cutting ma-

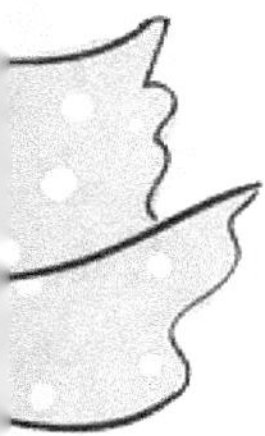

terials such as paper, thinner acetate, vinyl, transfer, tracing paper, and other materials.

- Premium blade (slightly golden) - has more extended durability than the traditional Ponta Fina.

- Fabric Blade (light pink) - for thinner fabrics. It is the same as the Ponta Fina blade, but the holder's color is different so that you can identify each one's function. In this way, you preserve the cutting edge and help to prolong the durability of your blades.

- Deep Cut Blade - For materials up to 1.7mm, it cuts EVA, thin cork, among other thicker materials, precisely.

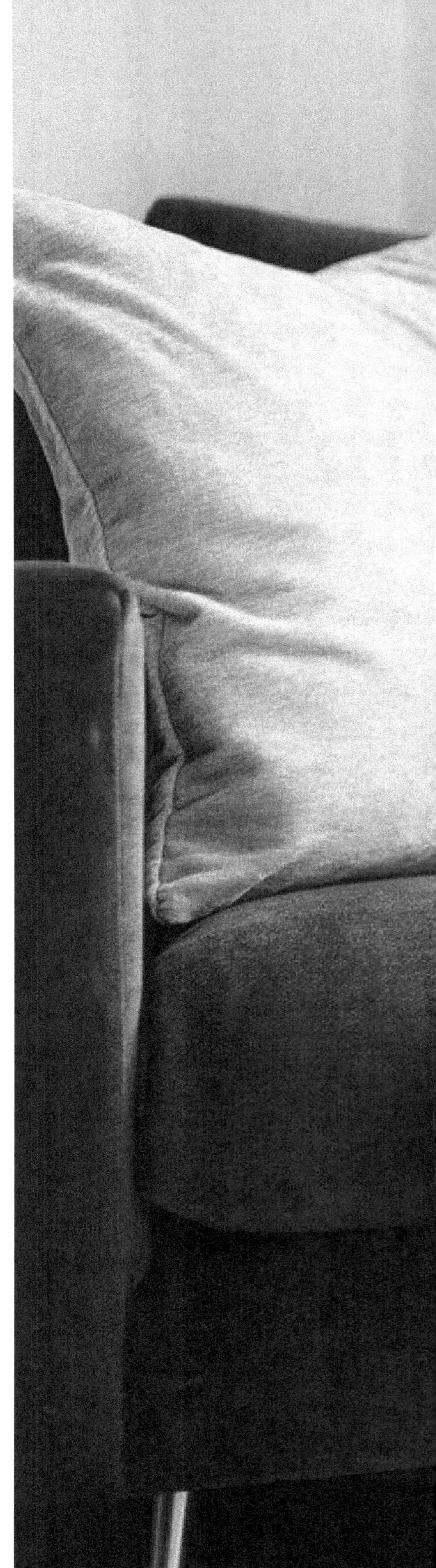

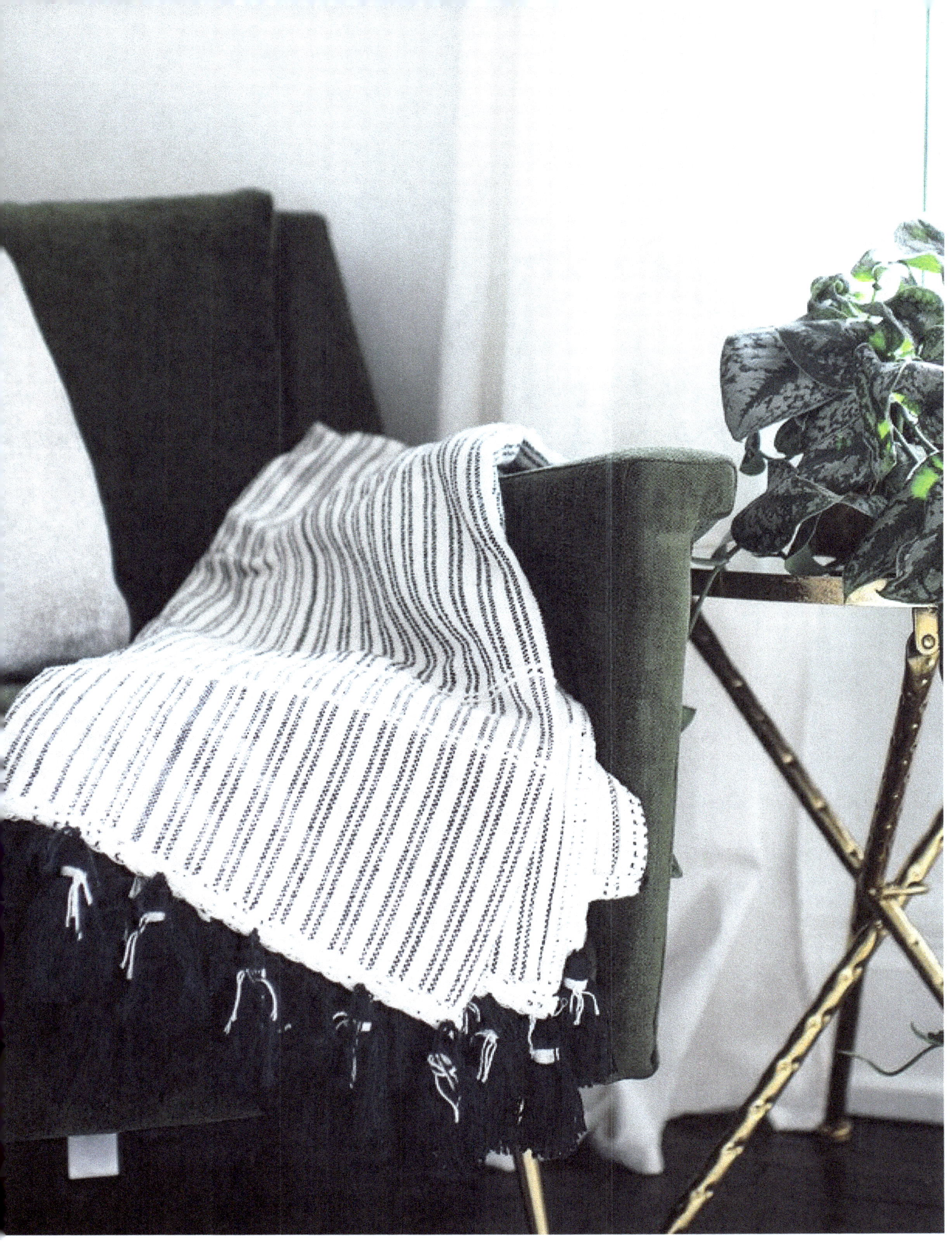

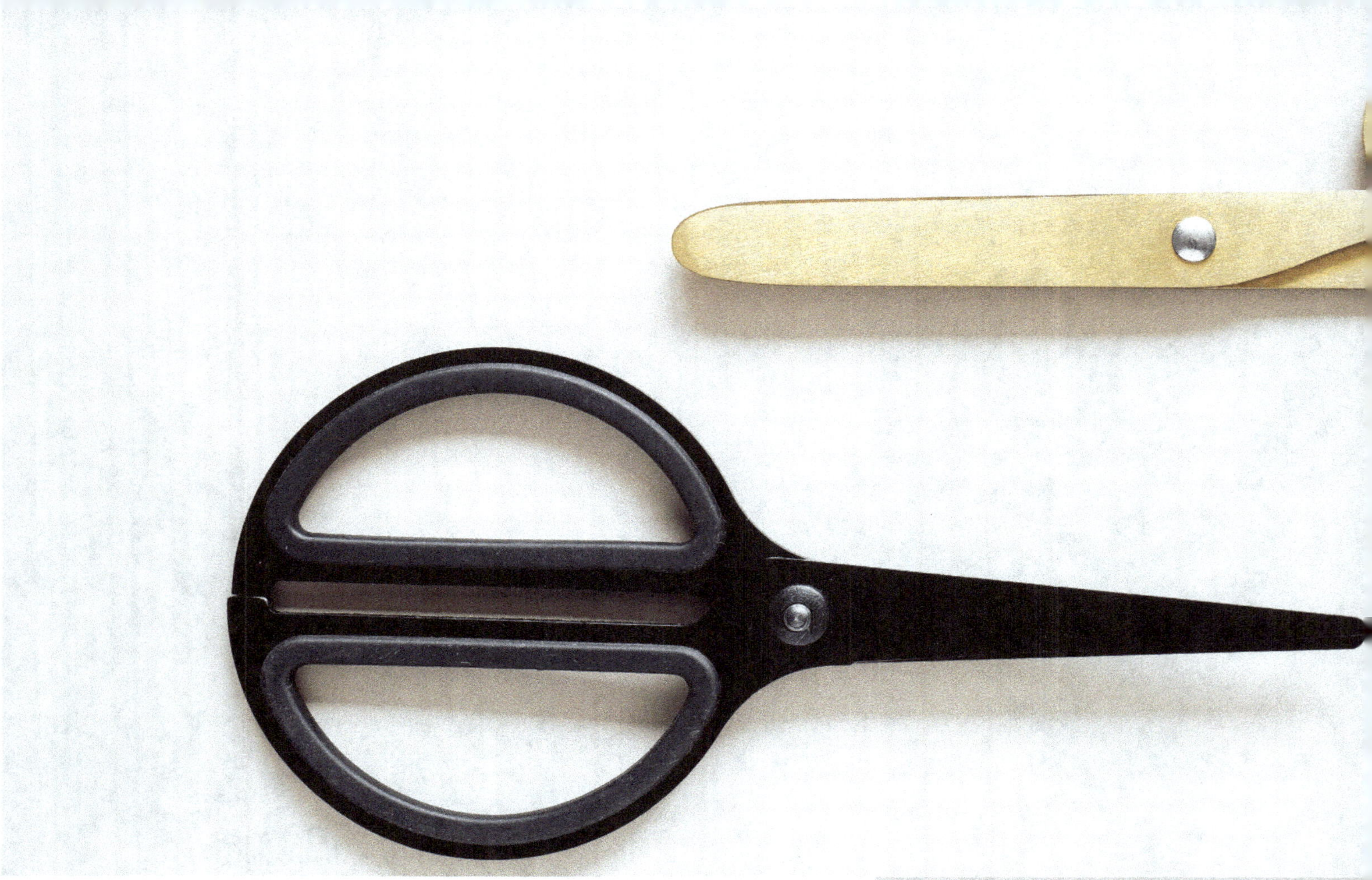

Changing the blades is very simple and cost-effective, even better because once you have the support, you only need to purchase the tip, that is, the blade!

Other tools and accessories will also give your pieces a special touch.

You know that perfect continuous crease, beautiful to live in? We have here, yes, sir!
The person responsible for it is an accessory tool called Crease Pen. Therefore, its role is essential to folds in boxes, invitations, or even extraordinary detail to the project. It suppor-

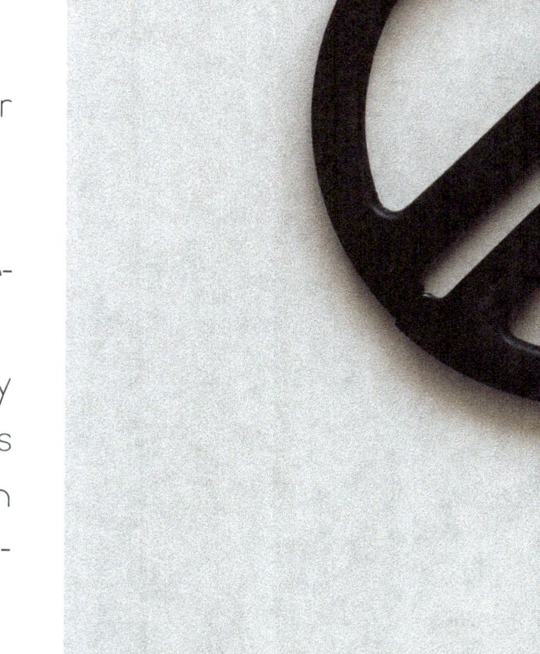

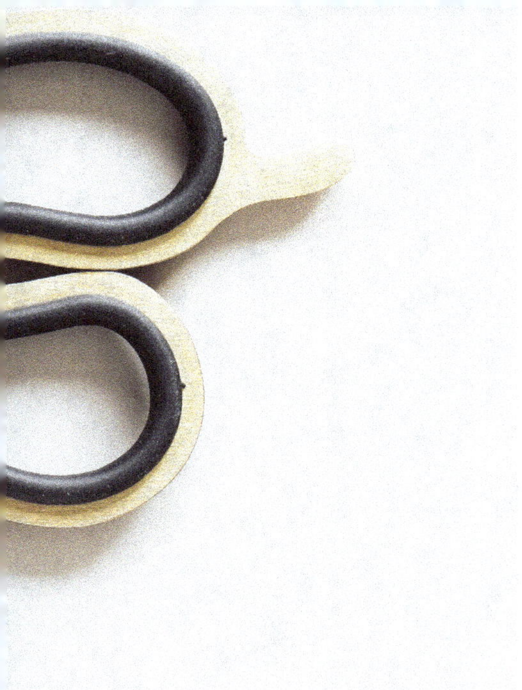

ts "A" on the cart's left side while the blade supports "B."

Pens can also be great allies to your creativity. Like the crease pen, Cricut pens are used in the "A" support of the cart.

Cricut has several types: Fine point, medium point, with sublimation ink, and even washable pen for fabrics. Yes! You draw, sew your piece, wash it, and the paint comes out, and the finish of your work is perfect!

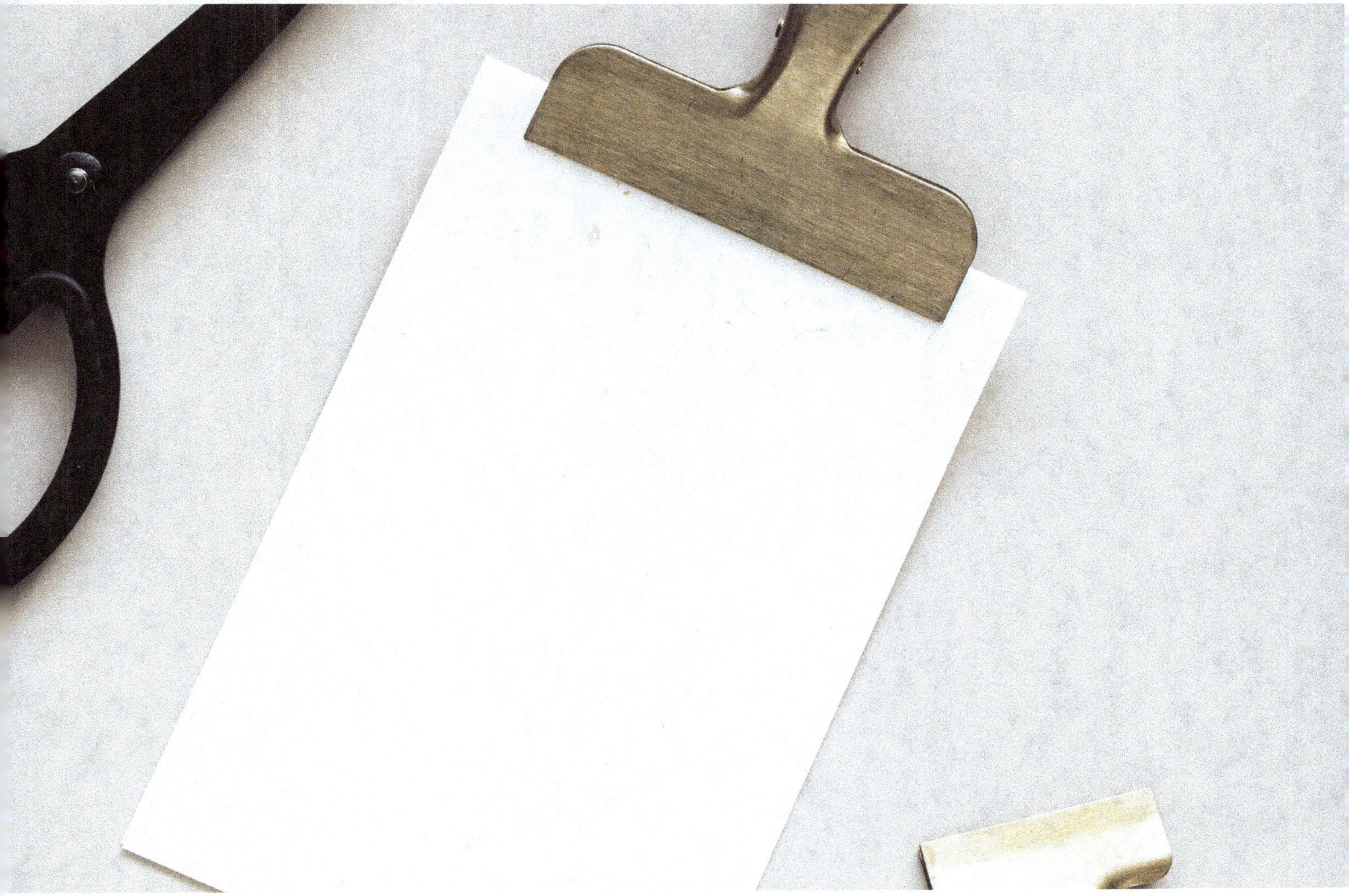

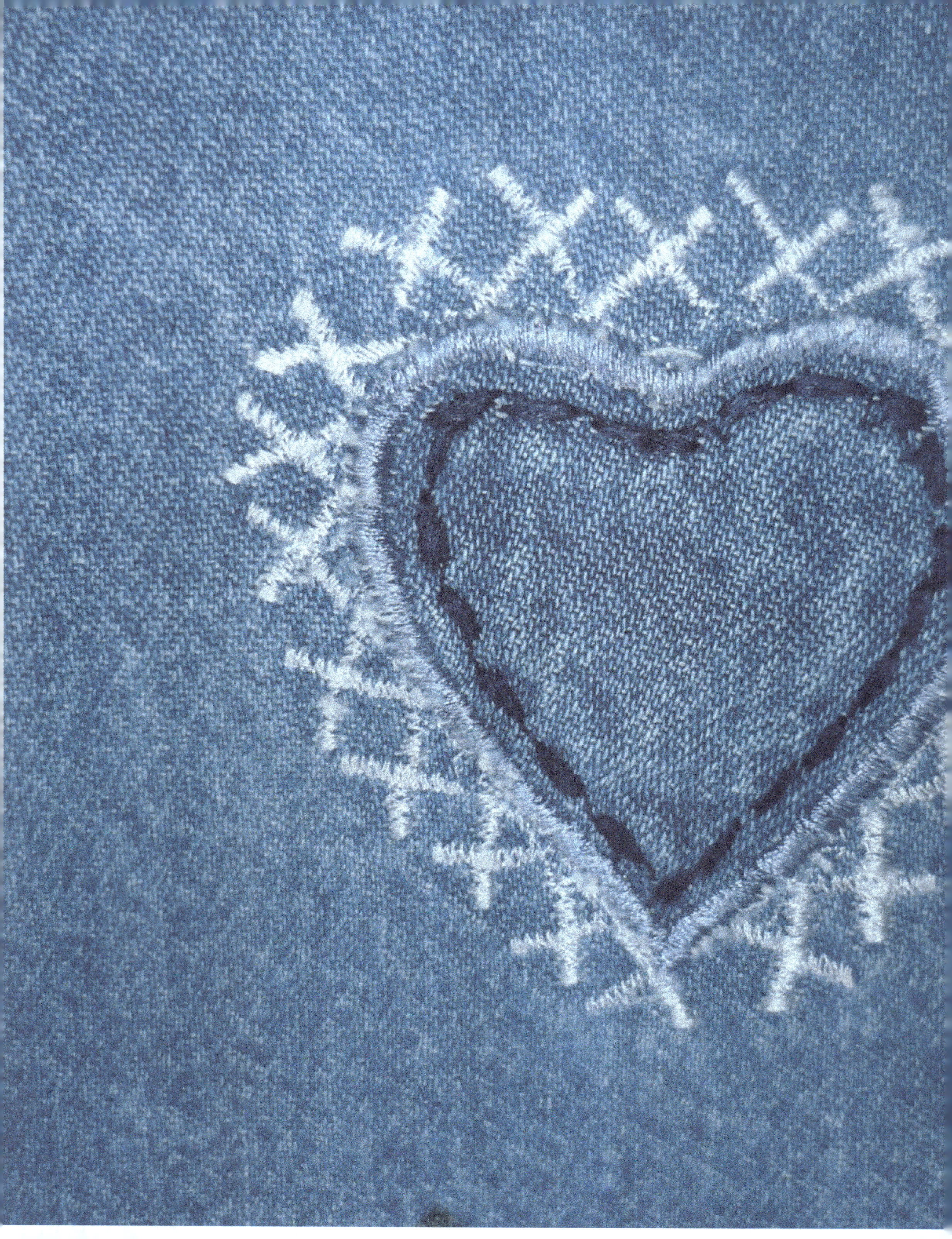

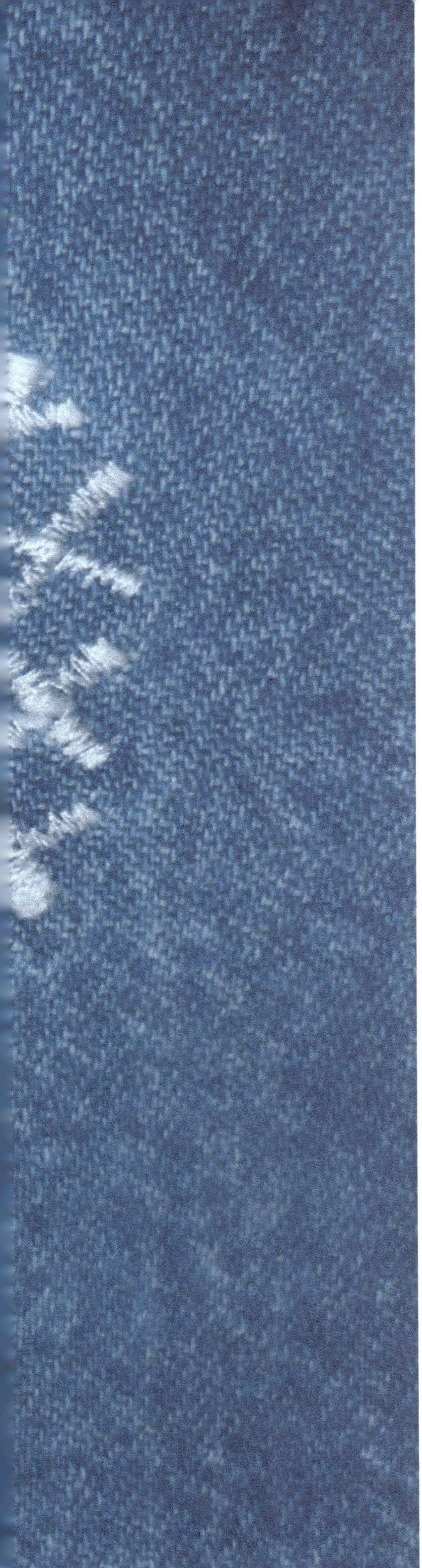

Personalized Ideas for Cricut

Cricut Explore Air 2 is an equipment that helps a lot in some or all stages of creative work such as Sewing, Scrapbook, Party Scrap, Home Decor, Stamping, Custom Stationery, Making Stickers, Making EVA pieces. It also helps who works with Painting because you can make stencil your way very personalized with it.

terials such as paper, thinner acetate, vinyl, transfer, tracing paper, and other materials.

- Premium blade (slightly golden) - has more extended durability than the traditional Ponta Fina.

- Fabric Blade (light pink) - for thinner fabrics. It is the same as the Ponta Fina blade, but the holder's color is different so that you can identify each one's function. In this way, you preserve the cutting edge and help to prolong the durability of your blades.

- Deep Cut Blade - For materials up to 1.7mm, it cuts EVA, thin cork, among other thicker materials, precisely.

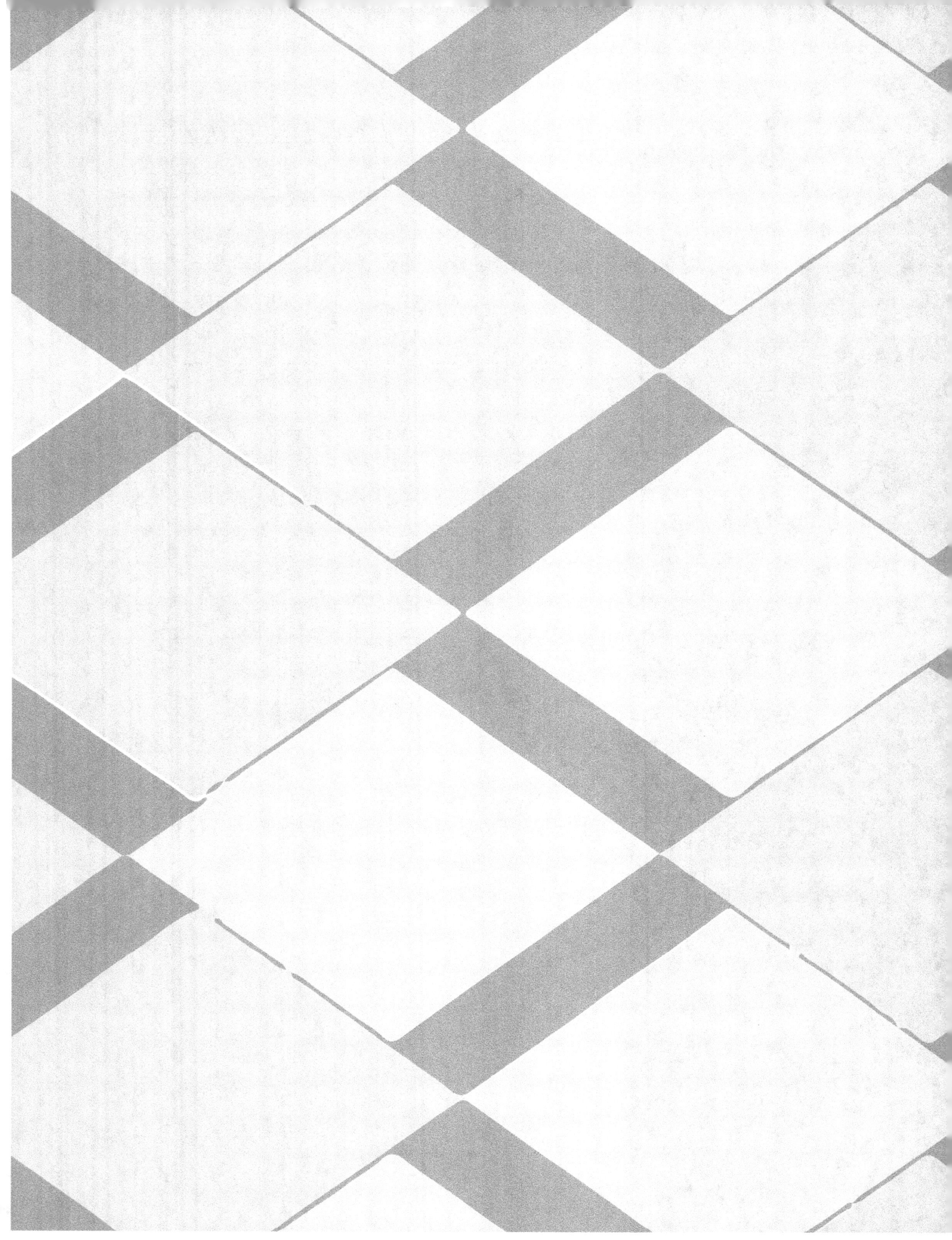

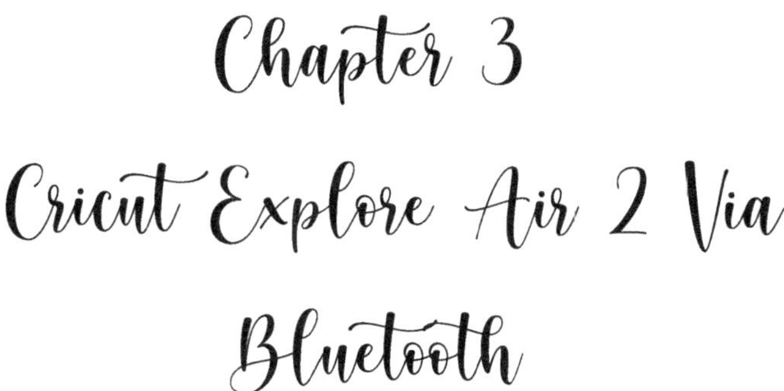

Cricut Explore Via Bluetooth

However, remember that this form of connection is optional but very useful for those who do not have much space to leave many wires on the table or bench where they work. Therefore, you can even work with the device away from Cricut, considering a maximum distance between 3m to 4.5m. First, to use Bluetooth, your computer must also have this device. Most of them already come with Bluetooth.

* Attention! The following steps and images were demonstrated using Windows 10. If you use another Windows operating system and need help, contact us.

To check if your computer already has Bluetooth, right-click on the "Start" button and click on the "Device Manager" option.

Therefore, if Bluetooth is listed among the

options, it means that your computer already has it.

However, if Bluetooth does not appear in the list and want to use it, you can buy a Bluetooth Dongle device to allow your computer's configuration with other equipment via Bluetooth.

Remember: if you don't have Bluetooth installed on your computer, that doesn't stop you from using your Cricut Explore Air 2. Just connect it via USB cable and be happy! :)

Now that we know whether your computer has Bluetooth or not close the Device Manager.

If your computer already has Bluetooth installed, it's time to set it up!

How to Set Up Bluetooth

1. Turn on your Cricut Explore Air 2.
2. Click on the search bar (next to the "Start" button) and type "Bluetooth."
An option called "Bluetooth and Other Device Settings" will appear. Click on it.
3. After that, check if the "Bluetooth"

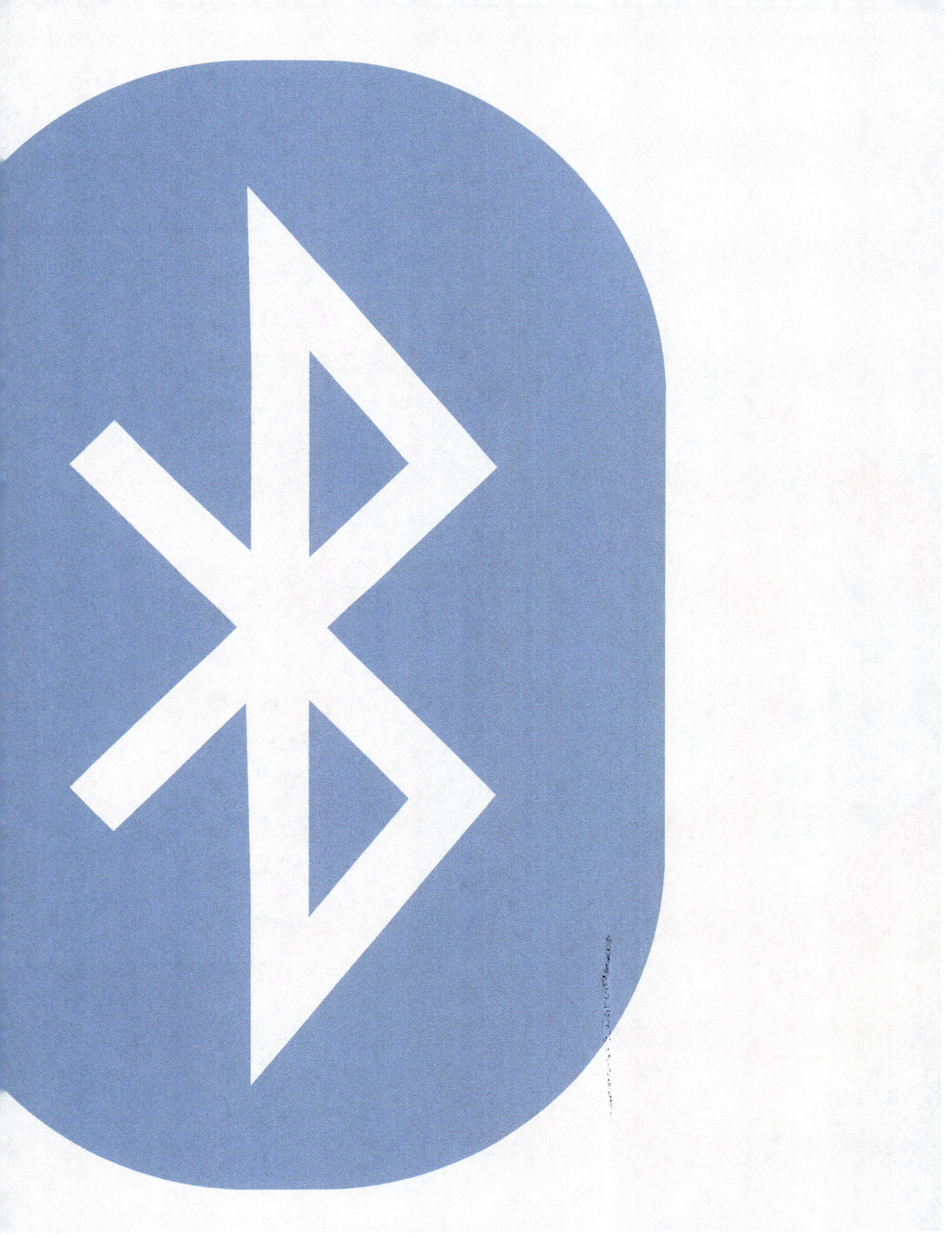

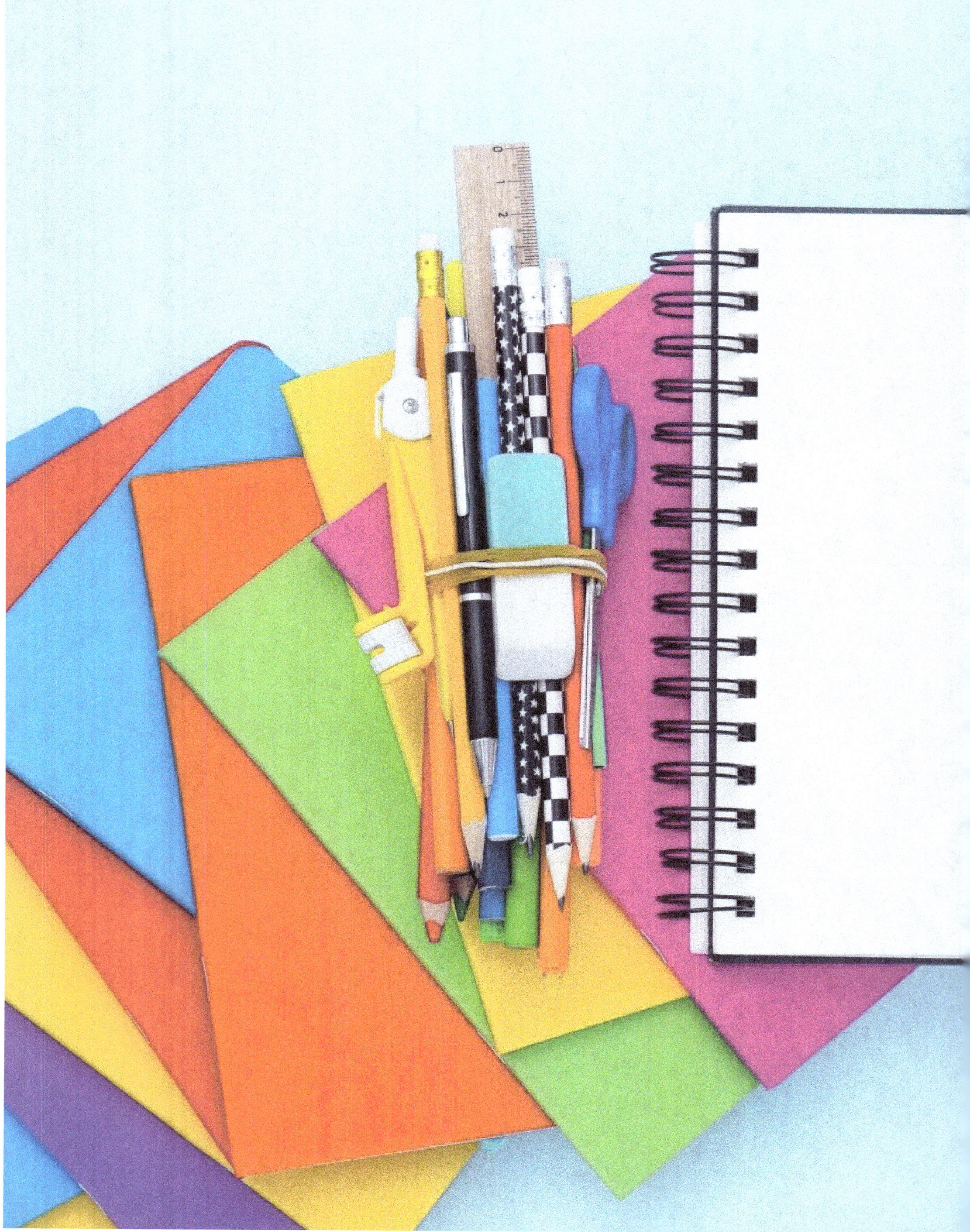

option is "Enabled." If not, you must activate it.

4.   Click on "Add Bluetooth or another device."

5.   Select the option where you have Bluetooth and wait. That's because your computer will automatically detect your Cricut Explore Air 2, and also other devices that work via Bluetooth that are around.

It is usual for Cricut Explore Air 2 to appear in the list as Audio. Therefore, if you have more than one Cricut device, you can identify them using the code on your device; you can find it on the serial number tag at the bottom of your Cricut Explore Air 2.

Blades, pens, and crease tool compatible with both machines:

•   Fine Point Blade, the standard blade, can cut materials up to 1.1 mm thick.

•   Bonded-Fabric Blade that has a pink color. Its function is the same as the Thin Point Blade. However, it has a different color so that they do not mix. In this way, the cutting edge will be preserved since they should only be used in their respective material. It can cut materials up to 1.1 mm thick.

•   Deep Cut Blade is a black blade that cuts materials up to 1.7 mm thick. However, if the material is very hard, like chipboard, it may not miss.

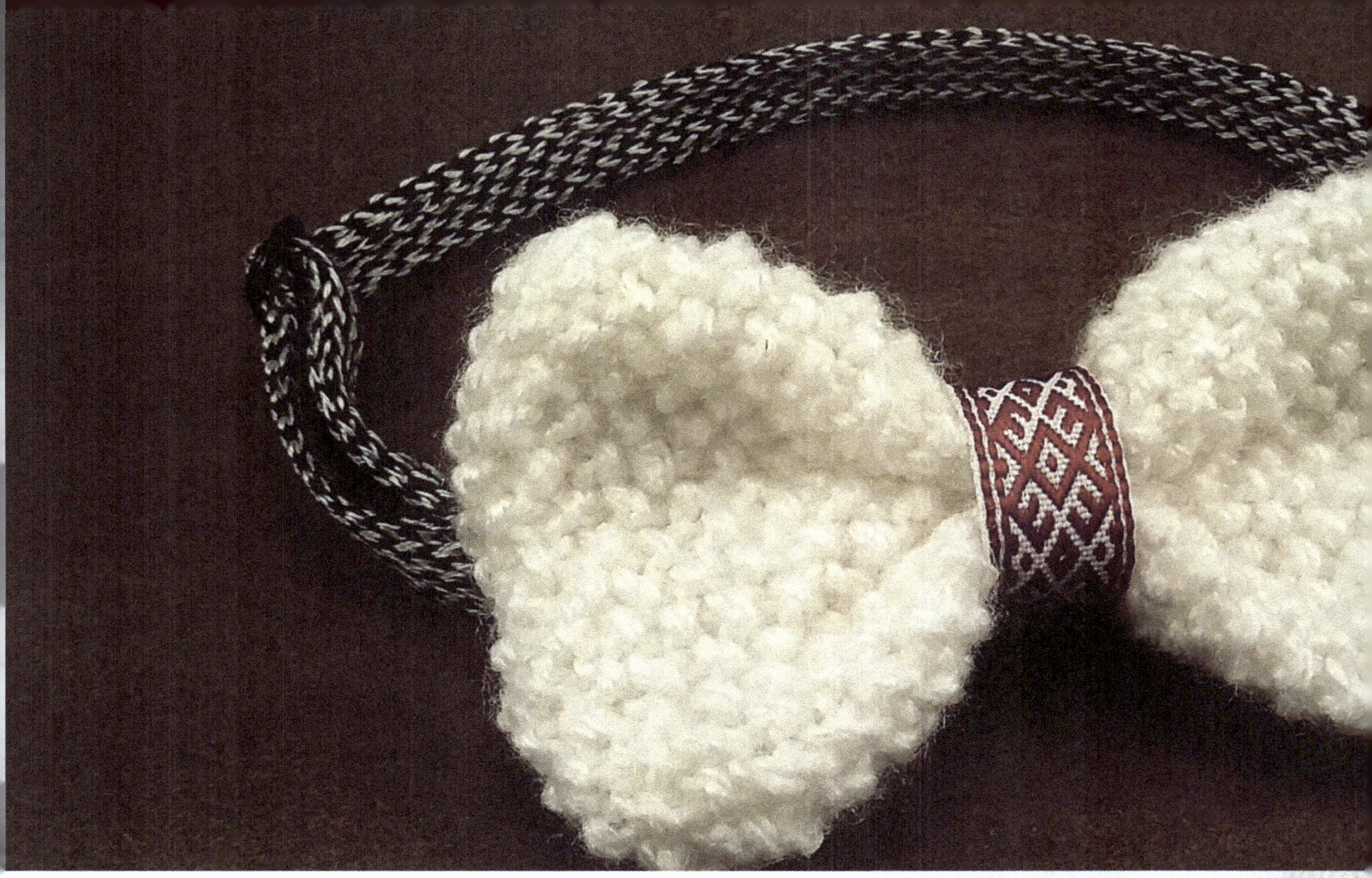

· Premium blade (Premium Fine Point Blade) with a slightly golden color can cut materials up to 1.1 mm thick. However, it has more outstanding durability.

· Fine, extra-fine, and medium-tipped pens. They are from Cricut itself, and you can find them in different colors.

· Crease Tool or Pen: accessory purchased separately to create the design

The two machines also use the same cutting bases with sizes 30 x 30 cm and 30 x 60 cm. It is necessary to be attentive since each floor is to be used with a type of material. Below, I explain to you which material should

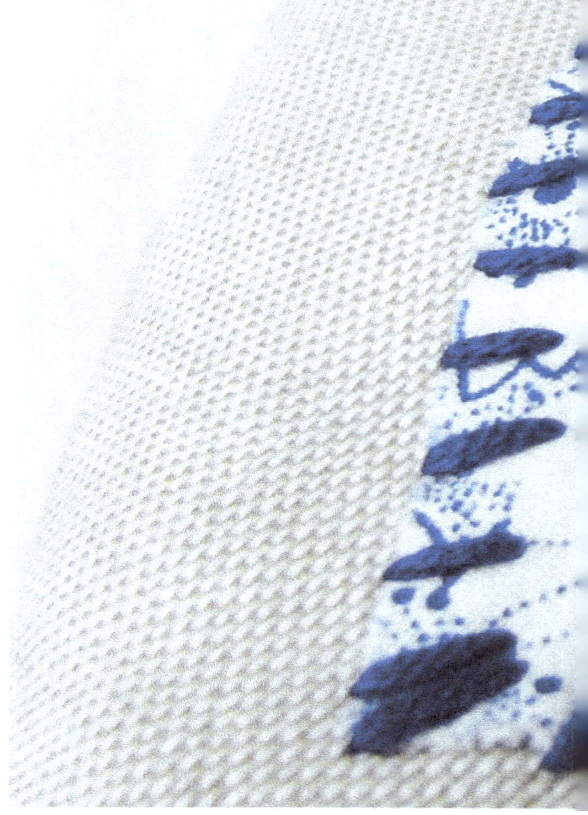

be used with every kind of base.

- Light Fixation Base (LightGrip Mat): for cutting more lightweight materials such as thin cardboard and tissue paper, for example. It has a light blue color.
- Standard Base (StandardGrip Mat): green. They are used for cutting heavy paper such as scrap and color plus forms, for example, vinyl, transfers and adhesive documents, and more.
- Strong Fixation Base (StrongGrip Mat): Its color is lilac and was developed to cut heavier cardboard, glitter paper, magnetic blanket, fabric with a heat-stabilizing / stabilizer base,

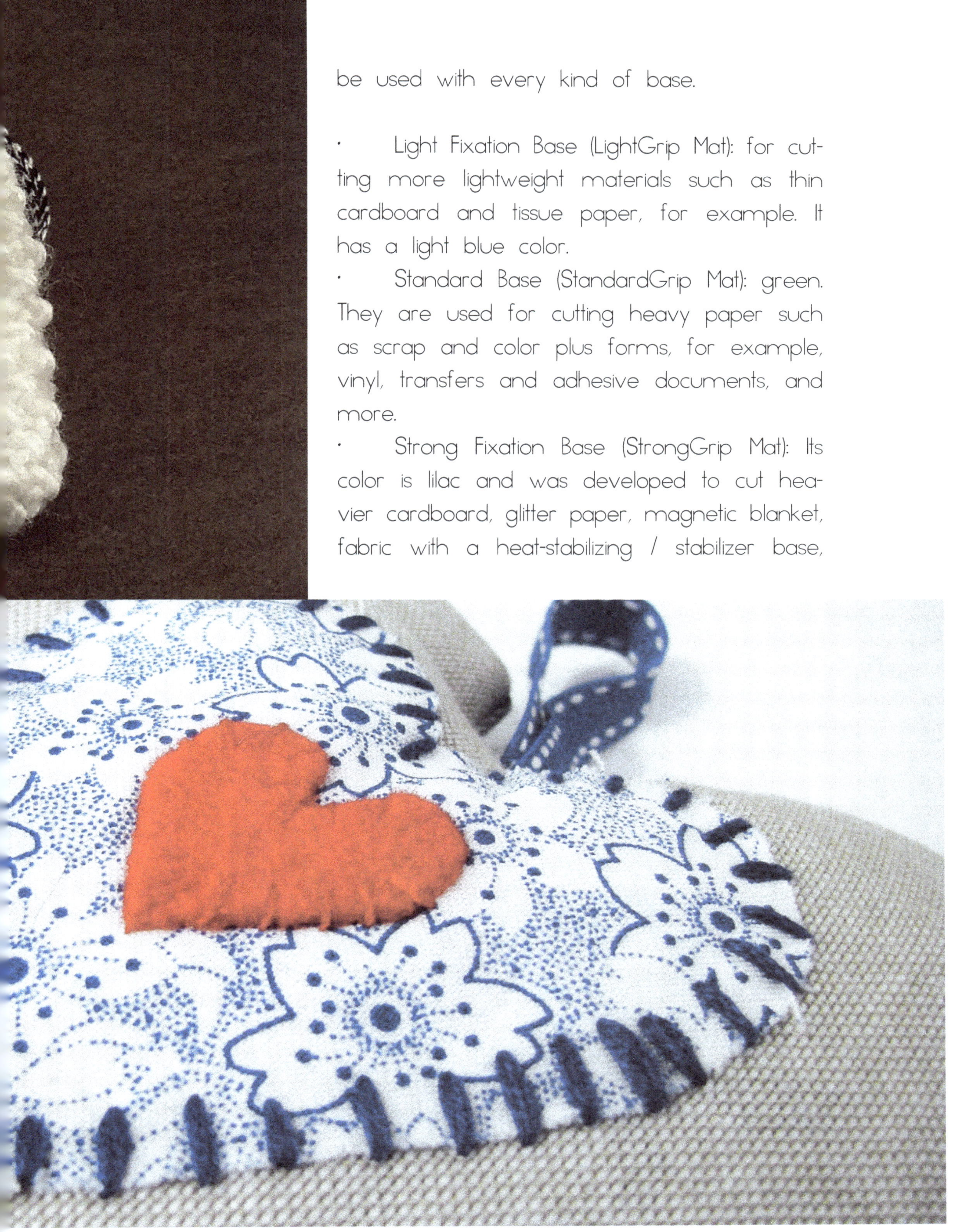

chipboard, among other thicker materials or that need a stronger fixation for cutting.

·	Fabric Cutting Base (FabricGrip Mat): in light pink, designed for cutting the most diverse fabrics using both the fabric blade and the rotary blade (exclusive to Cricut Maker).

Chapter 4
What Cricut Explore Air 2 Can Cut?

Paper	Vinyl	Iron-On
Cardstock	Fabric	Poster Board
Adhesive Foil	Aluminum Foil	Birch
Burlap	Canvas	Chalkboard Vinyl
Clear Printable Sticker Paper	Construction Paper	Copy Paper - 20lb
Cork, Adhesive-backed	Corrugated Cardboard	Craft Foam
Cutting Mat Protector	Deluxe Paper	Denim, bonded
Distressed Craft Foam,	Duct Tape	Embossed foil paper
Epoxy Glitter Paper	Faux Leather	Faux Suede
Felt	Foil Acetate	Grocery Bag
Chipboard	Magnetic Sheet	Notebook Paper
Paint Chip	Parchment Paper	Photo Paper

Silk, bonded	Vellum	Washi Sheet
Wax Paper	Wrapping Paper	Glitter Paper
Paper	Vinyl	Iron-On
Cardstock	Fabric	Poster Board
Adhesive Foil	Aluminum Foil	Birch
Burlap	Canvas	Chalkboard Vinyl
Clear Printable Sticker Paper	Construction Paper	Copy Paper - 20lb
Cork, Adhesive-backed	Corrugated Cardboard	Craft Foam
Cutting Mat Protector	Deluxe Paper	Denim, bonded
Distressed Craft Foam,	Duct Tape	Embossed foil paper
Epoxy Glitter Paper	Faux Leather	Faux Suede
Felt	Foil Acetate	Grocery Bag
Chipboard	Magnetic Sheet	Notebook Paper

Paint Chip	Parchment Paper	Photo Paper
Silk, bonded	Vellum	Washi Sheet
Wax Paper	Wrapping Paper	Glitter Paper

Chapter 5
How To Keep Cricut Explore Air 2 Machine Clean And Efficient

Want to enjoy your machine? Here are a few tips and tricks that will help you.

De-Tack Your Cutting Mat!

Your Cricut Explore Air will arrive with a cutting mat upon which you will put your projects before cutting. When purchased newly, the cutting mat is usually very sticky. I would advise that you prime the cutting mat before your first use. Priming makes it less sticky such that your paper projects do not get damaged. You prime the cutting mat by placing a clean, dry fabric over the cutting stock over the cutting mat and pulling it out again.

Keep Your Cutting Mat Clean

Use wipes to keep your cutting mat clean. Be careful with alcohol wipes as they could make the carpet lose stickiness. You can also

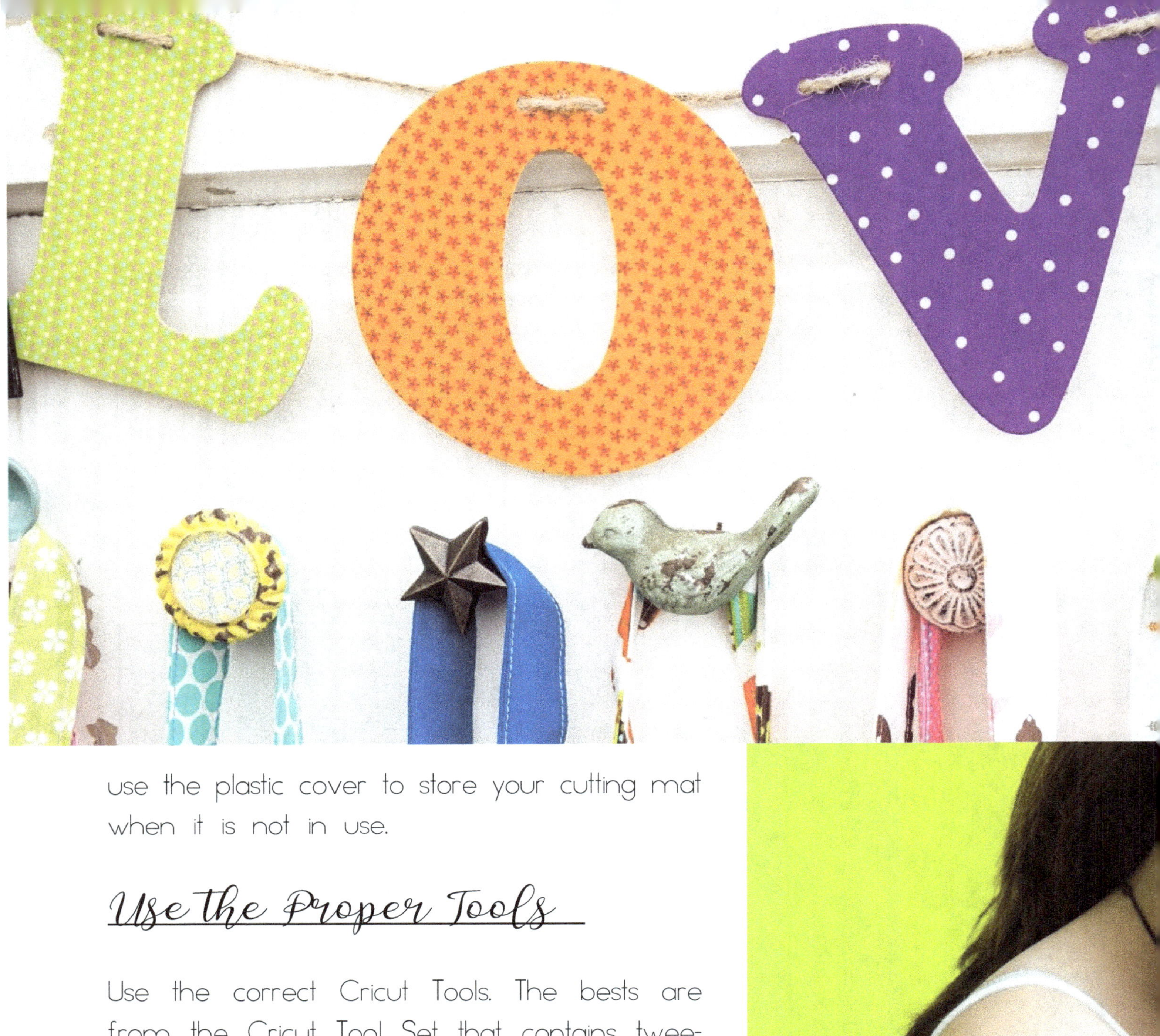

use the plastic cover to store your cutting mat when it is not in use.

Use the Proper Tools

Use the correct Cricut Tools. The bests are from the Cricut Tool Set that contains tweezers, scrapers, scissors, a spatula, and a weeding tool. These make work go very smoothly.

Start Your Cricut Journey with the Sample Project

It is best to start with the sample project and the material provided. The materials you will find in the package will be sufficient for you to create an initial sample project. Start with a simple sample project to have a feel of how the machine works.

Always Test Cuts

When carrying out projects, it is advisable to do a test cut before running the whole project. You can designate a simple amount to test run your settings before cutting material for the project. If the blade is not well set, the test cut will reveal it.

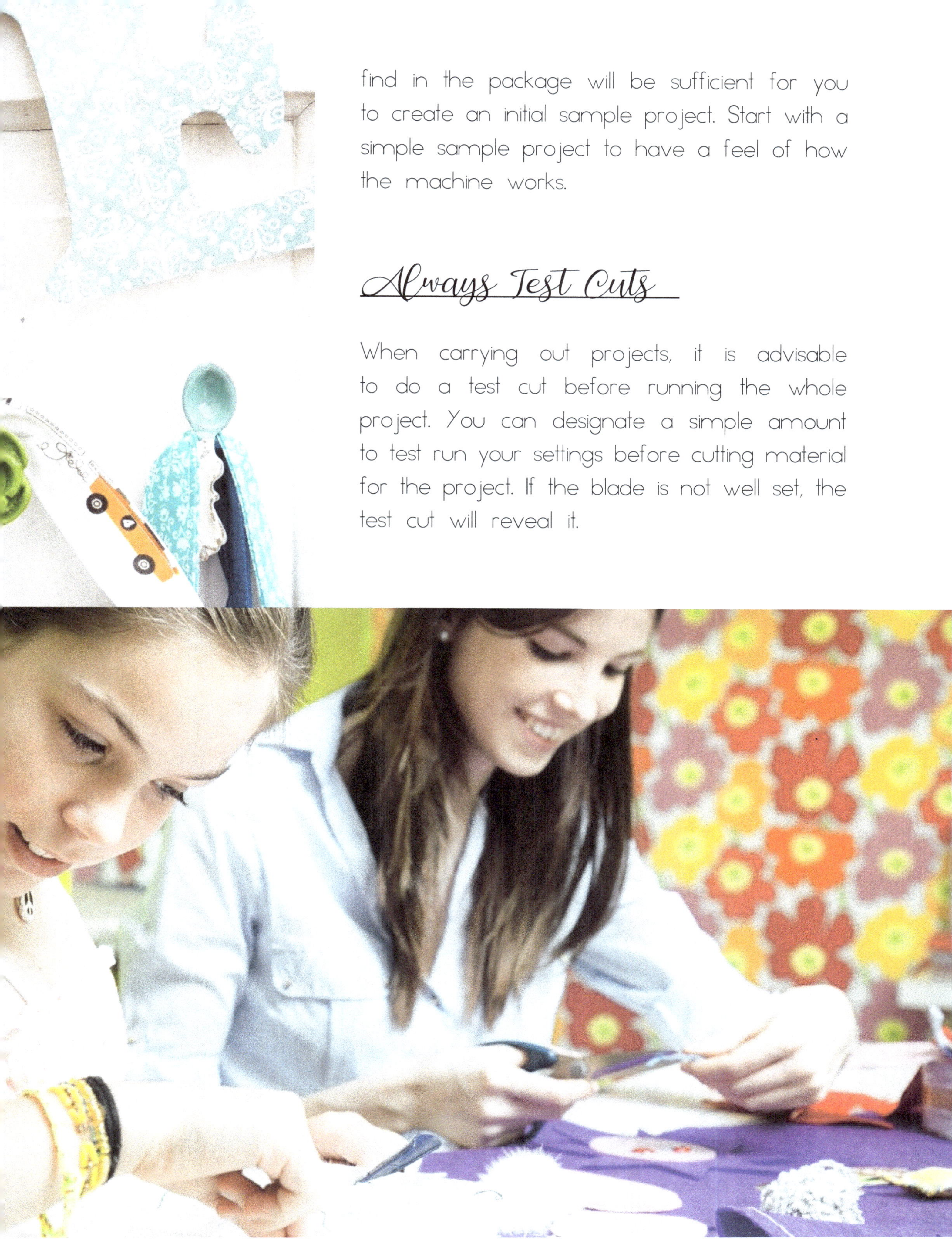

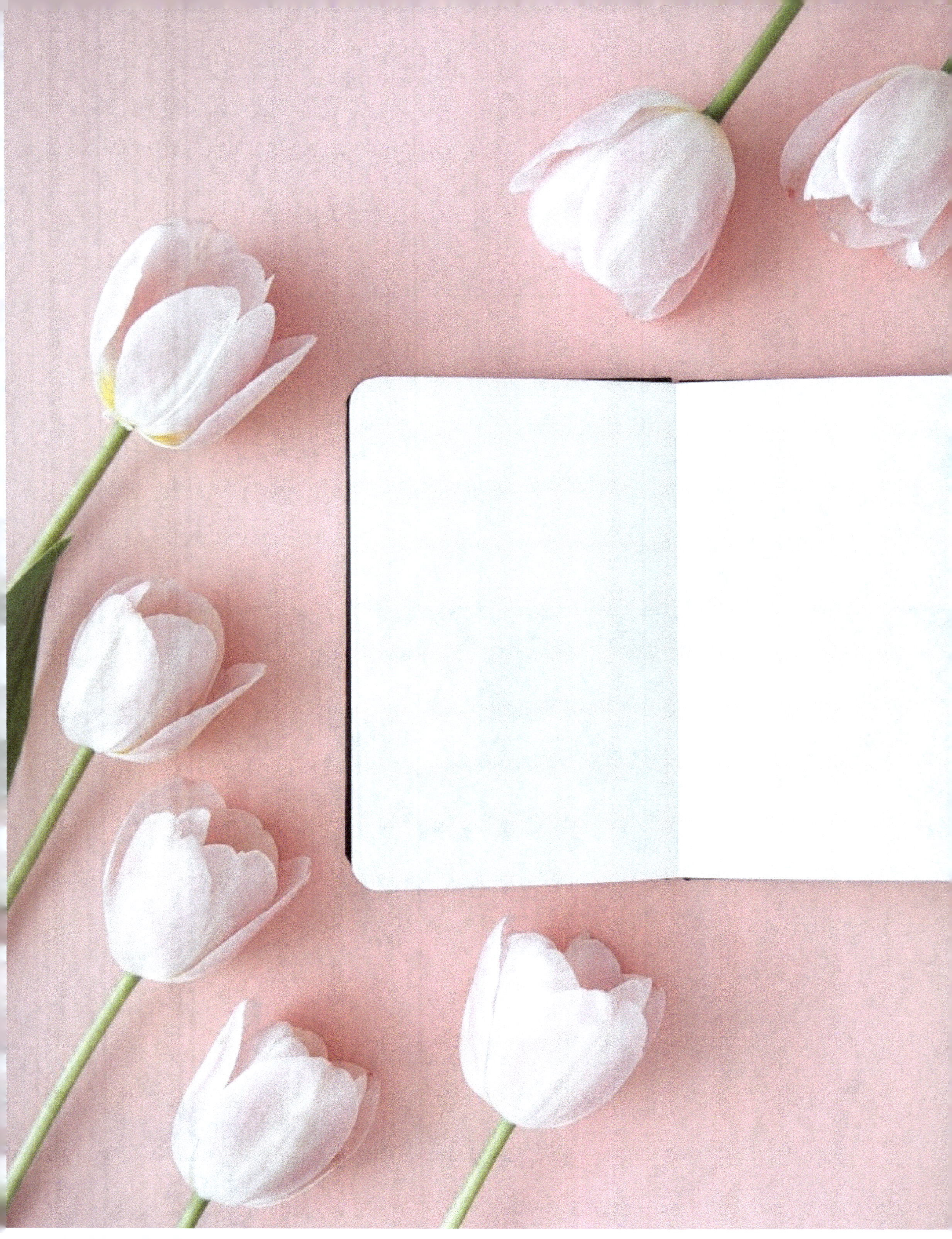

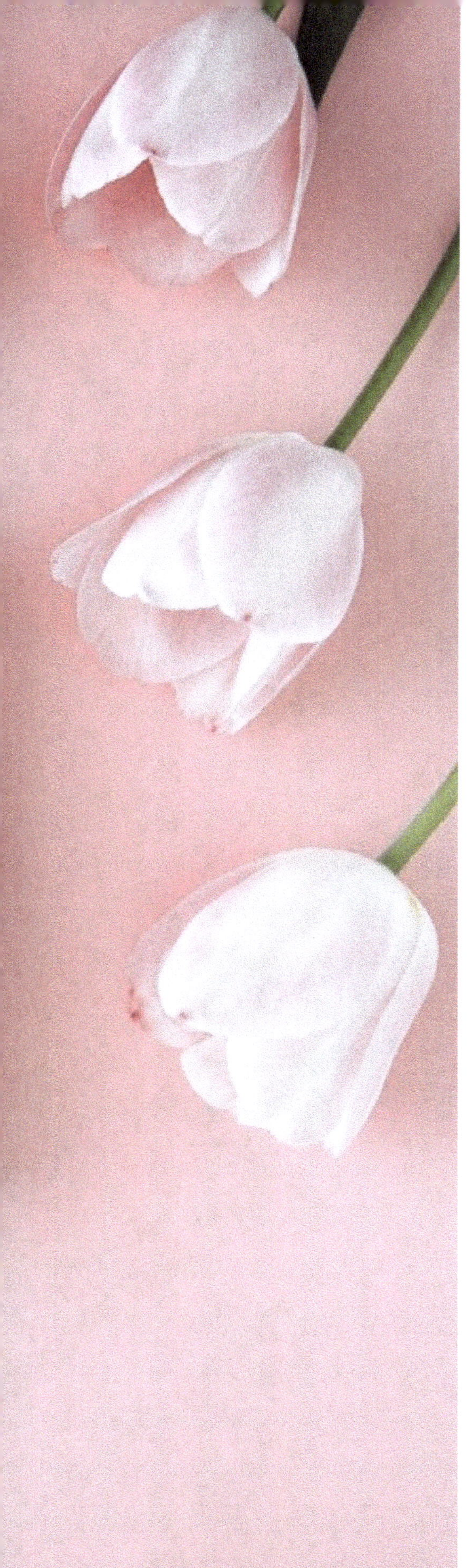

Replace Pen Lids After Use

Replace the pen lids when you are done using your pens. This prevents it from drying out. It is a good thing that Design Space sends a notification that reminds you to put the lid back on!

Link Your Old Cricut Cartridges

If you have cartridges you have used with your older machines, and you can still hook them up with your new device.

Bend the Cutting Mat to Get Materials off the Cutting Mat

To remove cut materials from the cutting mat (incredibly delicate Vinyl), you can bend the carpet away from the fabric. That way, you can use the spatula to help get the cut material off the cutting mat.

Use the Deep Cut Blade for Thicker Materials

Use the deep-cut blade to cut through thick materials. These materials could be leather, cardboard, or even chipboard. Get the edge and the blade housing.

Use Different Pens Where Necessary

Like you should use different blades for different materials, you should use other pens for different uses. There are additional pen adapters available which you can use with your machine.

Make Use of Free Fonts

There are many free fonts you can use. You can make use of these fonts for free instead of purchasing fonts on Cricut Access. When you identify a desired open front, download it, and install it on your computer. The font will appear on Cricut Design Space.

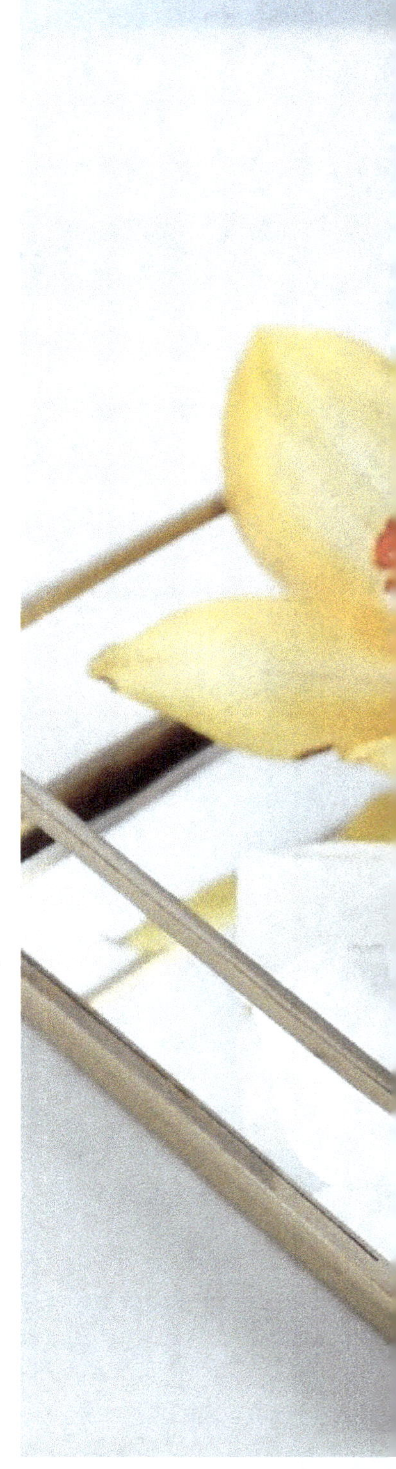

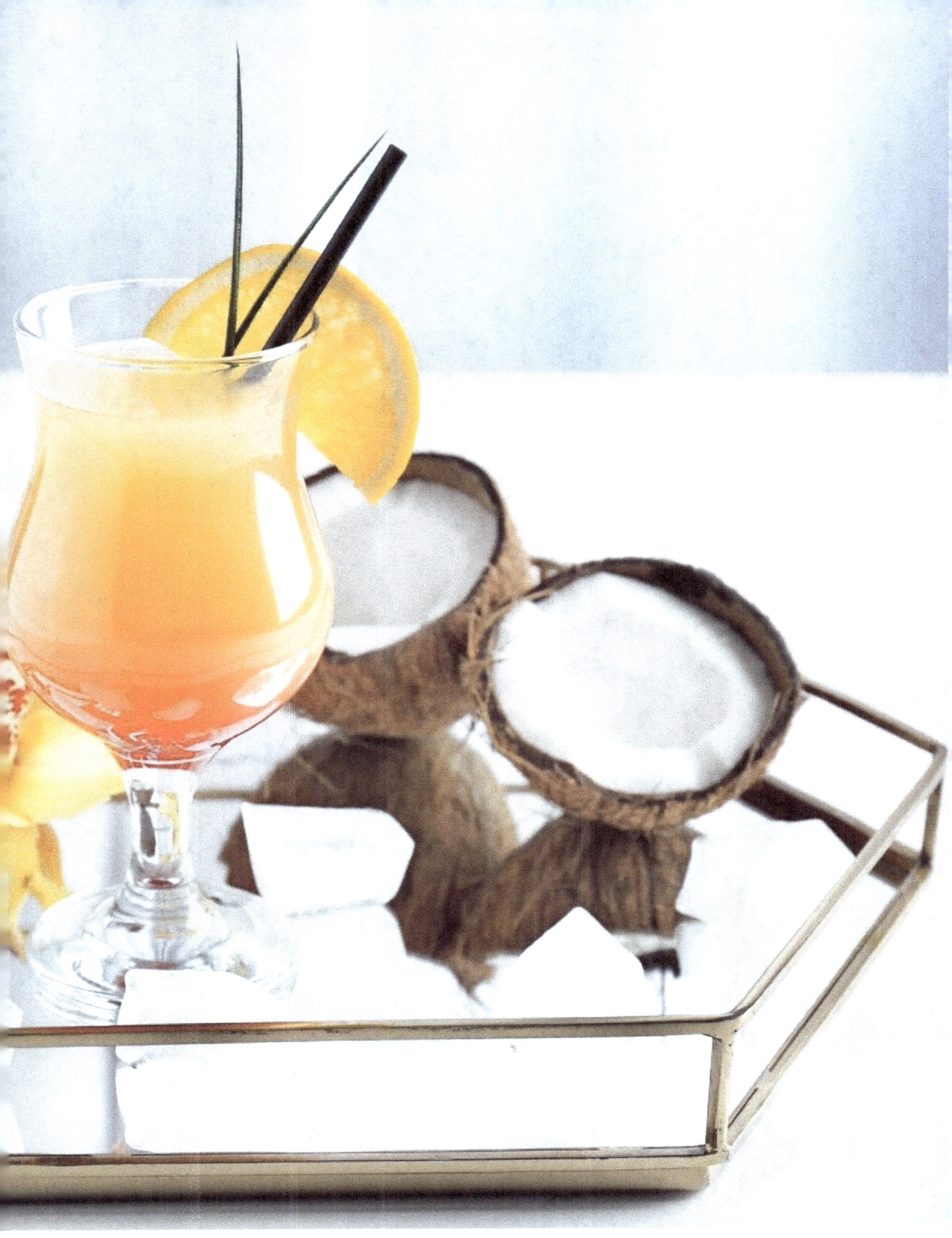

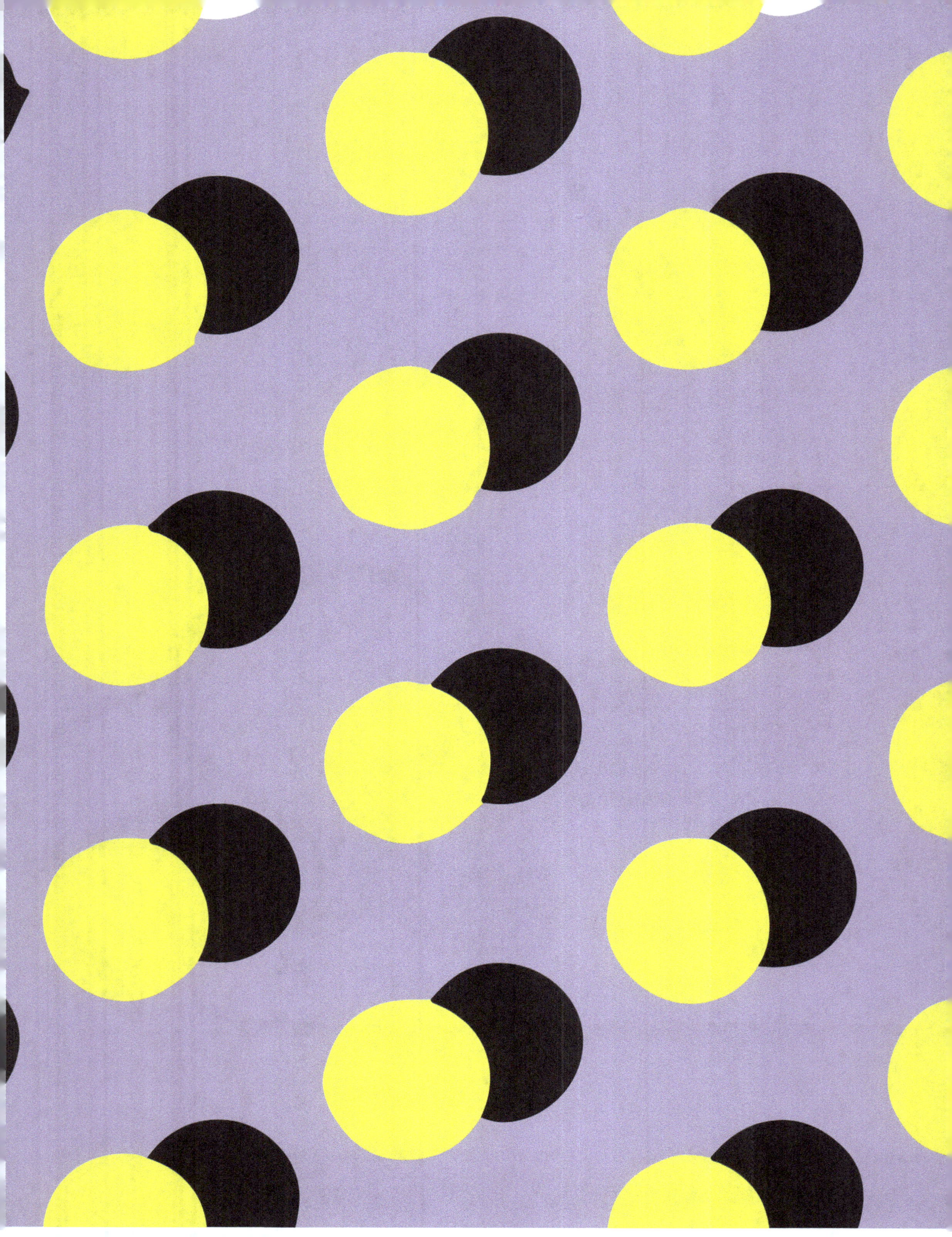

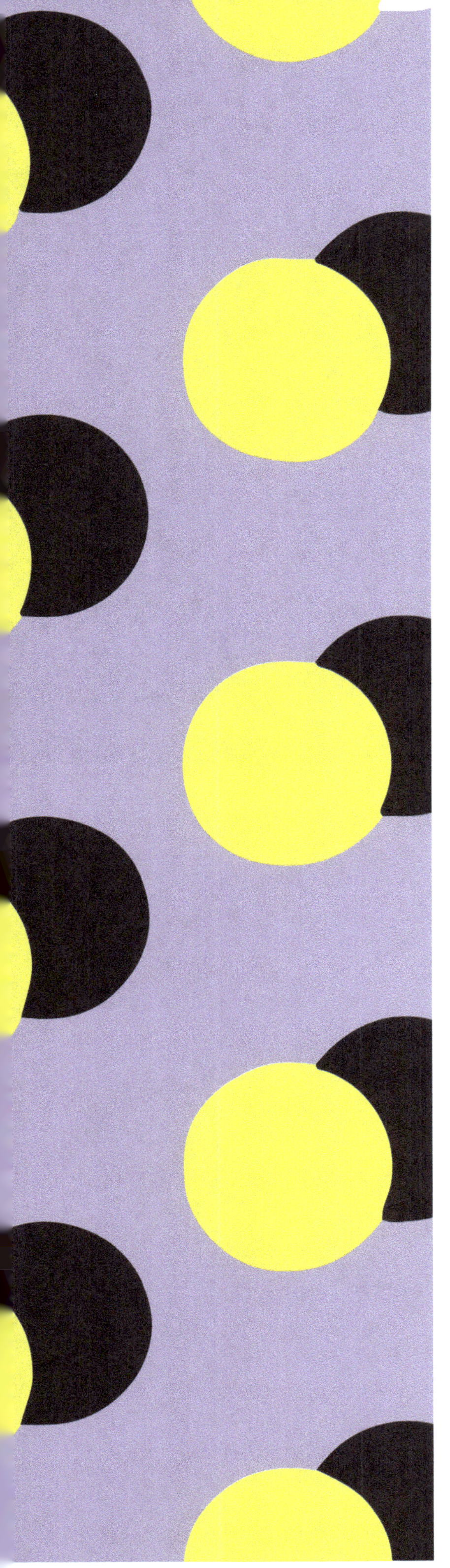

Use Different Blades for Different Materials

—

Do not use one single blade for all the different materials you will cut. For example, you can have one blade for cardboard, another for only leather, and one for vinyl. It is best to have different blades for different materials because each material wears differently on edge. A dedicated advantage will be best because it will be tuned to the peculiarities of each material.

Use Weeding Boxes for Intricate Patterns

When cutting delicate or intricate patterns, it is essential to use weeding boxes in the process. Create a square or rectangle using the square tool in Cricut Design Space and place it such that all your design elements are in it. Doing this makes weeding easier as all your design elements are grouped within the square or rectangle you have created.

Always Remember to Set the Dial

This sounds like stating the obvious setting the

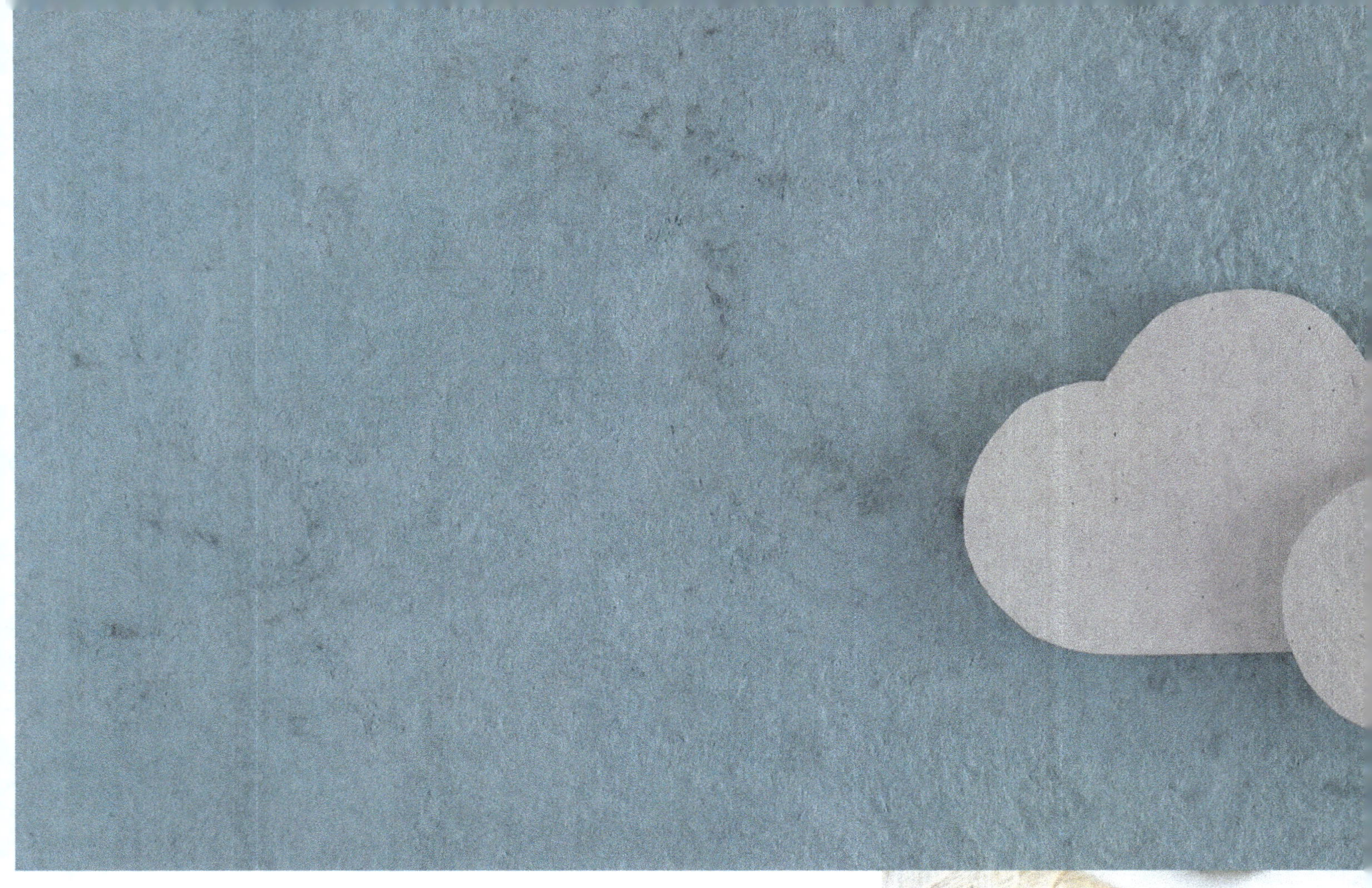

dial to the right material is something you can easily forget. The consequences of ignoring to set the dial to the appropriate material are range from damaged cutting mats to shallow cuts on the materials. You can prevent these by always putting the dial before cutting.

Other Tips & Tricks

Always clean your Cricut cutting mat after every project. Roll a lint roller over the Cricut mat to remove tiny leftovers of dirt and lint from the surface of the carpet.

To ensure that you do not regret your action

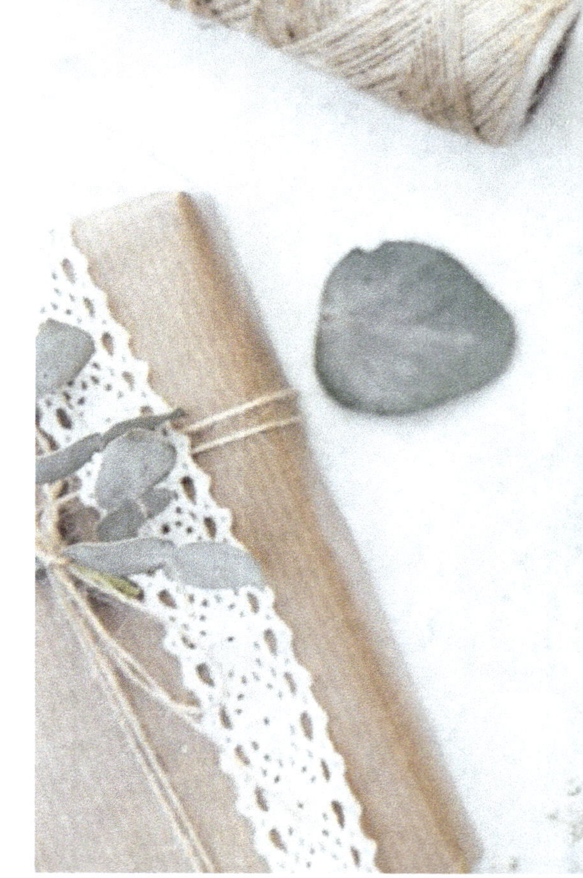

while using any Cricut machine, Cricut Explore Air 2 included a habit of always testing your material's cutting using a small piece of the material you wish to cut first before cutting the primary material. Watch out for these materials: wood, fabric, or felt because they present different challenges during the cut process.

When you want to detach your processed material from the cutting mat after unloading it, roll the Cricut mat backward away from the material instead of peeling it away from the Cricut mat.

Always organize your blades and knives in a separate compartment or container. This will

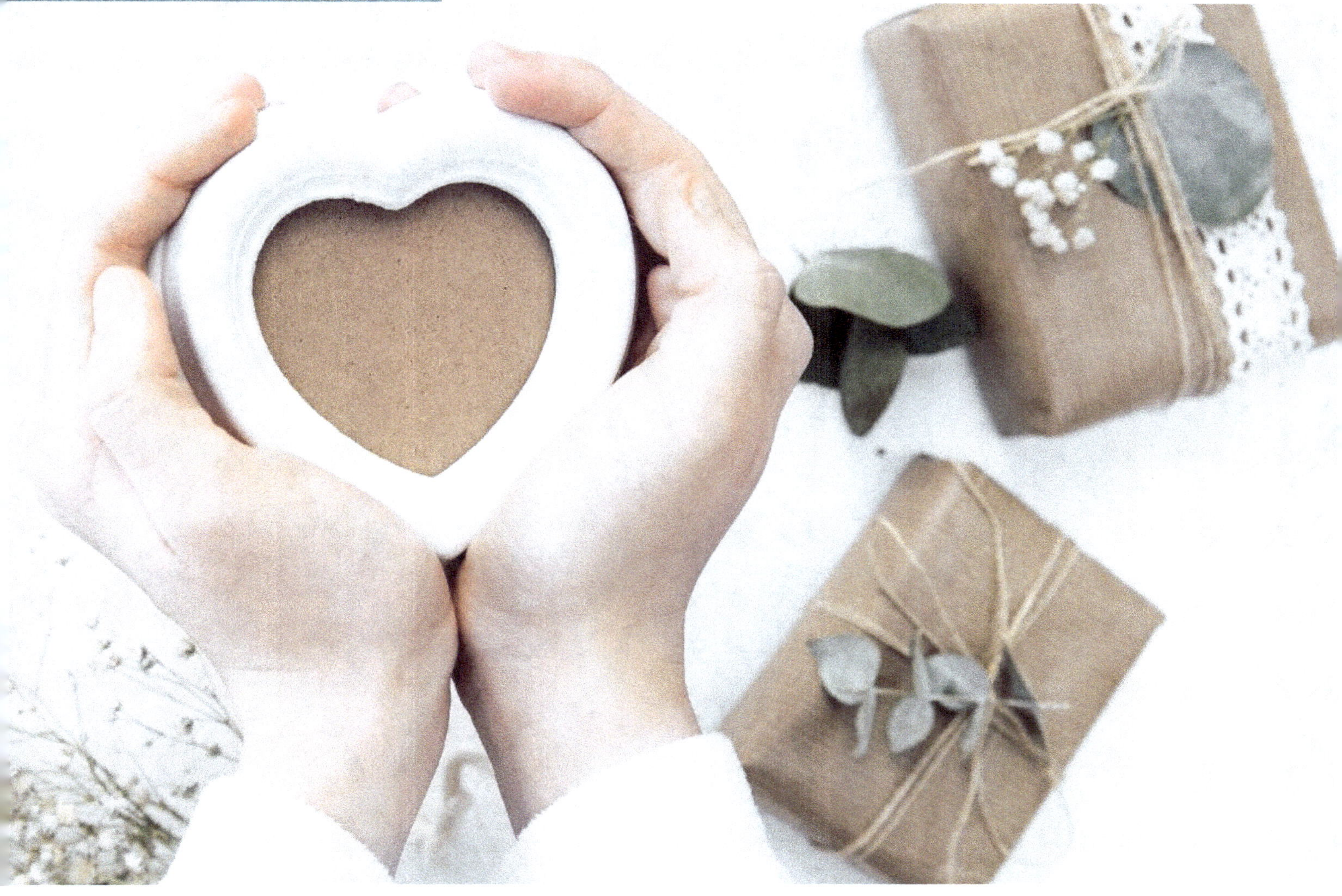

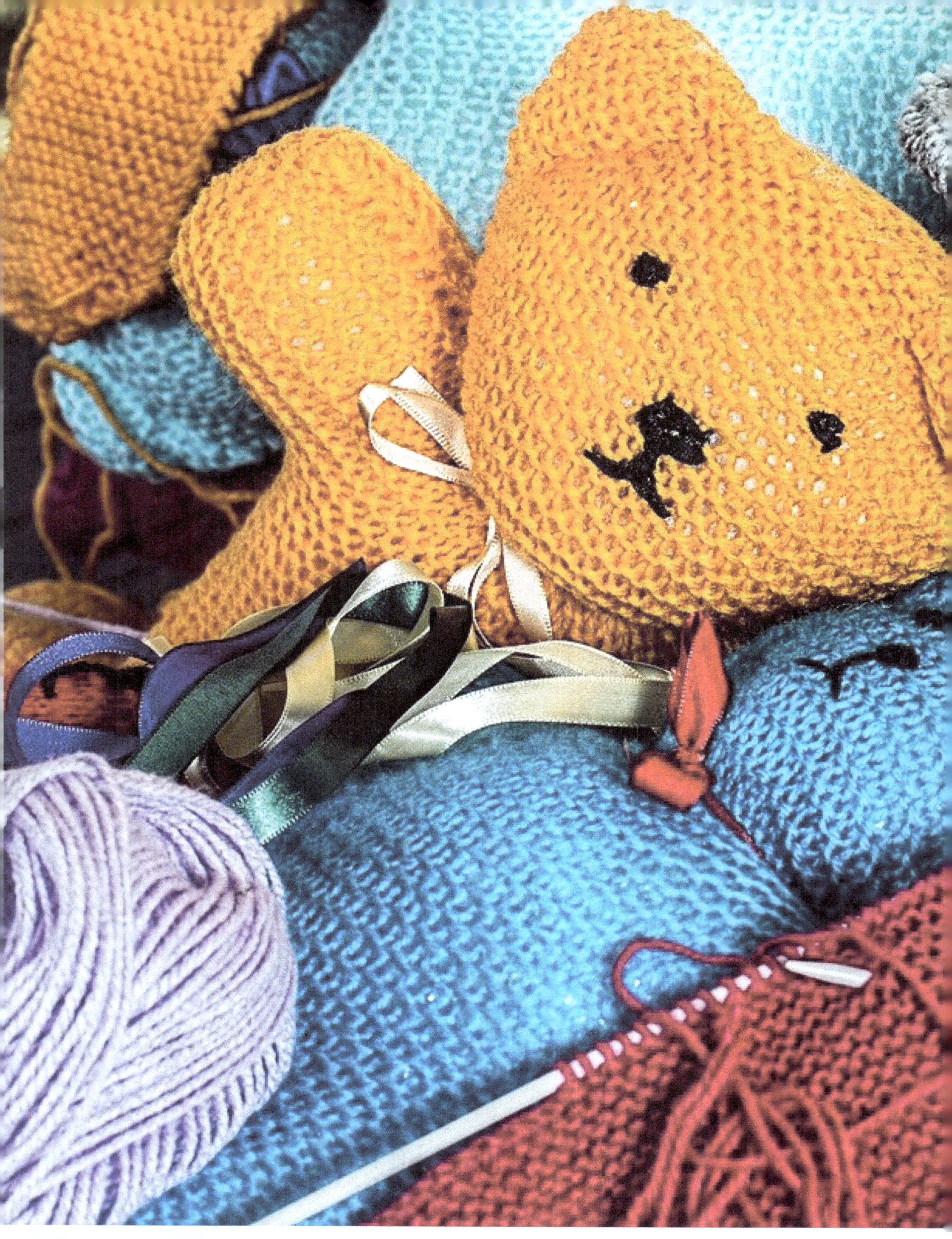

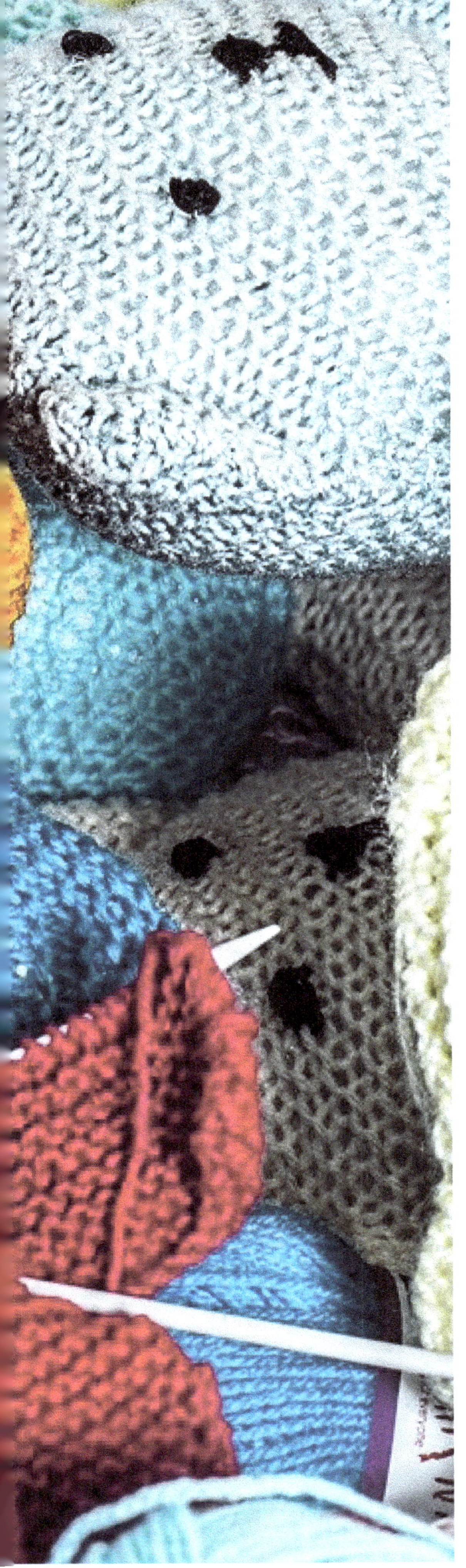

help you pick the correct blade or knife for a particular project because mixing them up may lead you to use an inappropriate edge for a project, resulting in blunting the blades or even outright damage.

Organize your Cricut tools so that they will not be flying everywhere around the project area to avoid messing up with your project or even causing you bodily harm. These tools include scissors, spatula, scoring tools, pic, weeding tools, etc.

You must keep your blades sharp every time so that you do not get your materials messed up while cutting and get them replaced when necessary.
Ensure that you dispose of the used ones properly to avoid injury to you and those around you, especially moms with little kids. I am sure you do not want your kids to get hurt from the blades.

Use this vital resource from the makers of Cricut Explore Air 2; their website Cricut.com where you are granted access to many YouTube videos and project ideas. If you need more help, search for information on Google

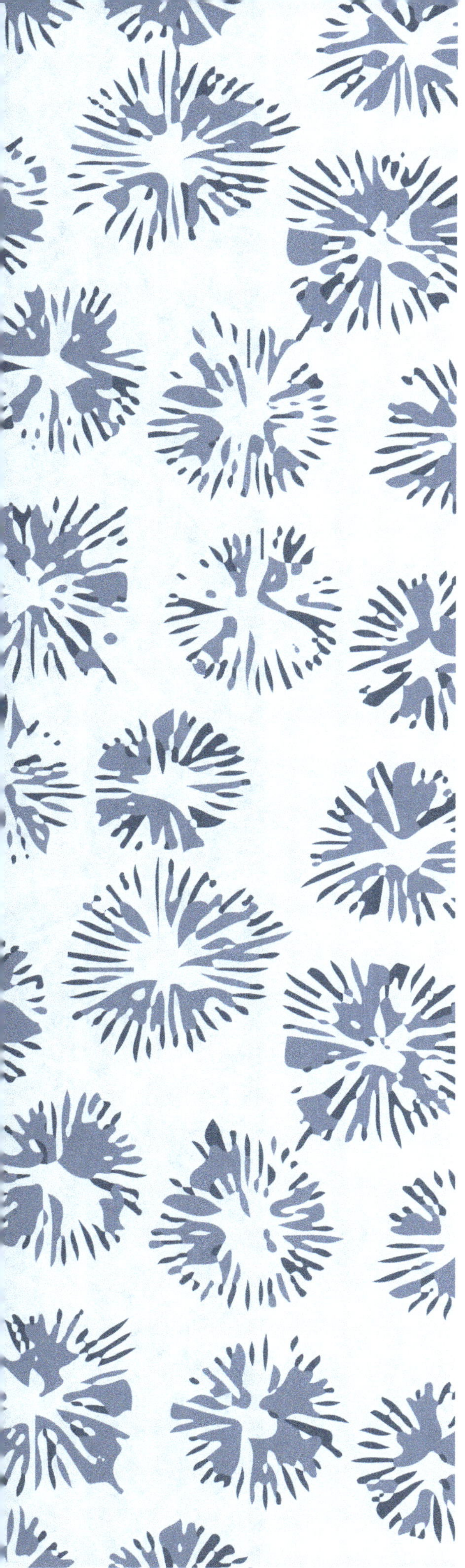

or Pinterest.

Using features such as fonts and a few projects on Cricut will cost you a few bucks, but you can cut this cost by subscribing to Cricut Access. With this, there is worry about cartridges, and all purchases will stay in your account.

If the cut edges of the material you are working on are rough and uneven, it merely means that the blade you are using is blunt. The solution is to replace the blade with another one.

If the cutting mat material moves while being cut, it means that your carpet is not sticky enough. The solution is to replace your carpet and the used cloth or use tape to hold your material firmly to the mat.

Chapter 6
Cricut Explore Air 2 Accessories And Tools

Essential Tools

Cartridge

The word cartridge may confuse you with printer cartridges. However, a Cricut cartridge is a physical cartridge used in older machines. It is a digital collection of designs that you purchase and keep for future use.

Each cartridge comes with a keyboard overlay and instruction booklet.
Cartridges are organized in themes. You can get licensed cartridges with premium artworks from Marvel, Disney, Pixar, Nickelodeon, Sesame Street, DC Comics, and Hello Kitty. You can buy these cartridges from Design Space or the Cricut website. These cartridges only work with Cricut software, and you will have to register

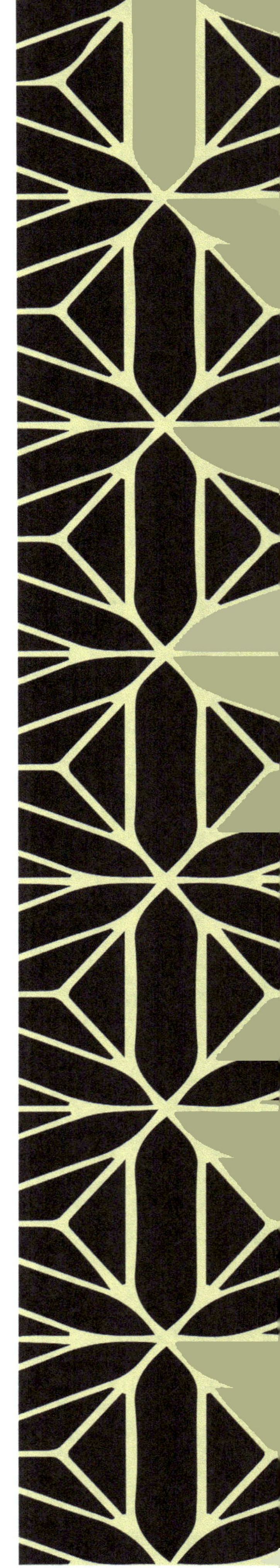

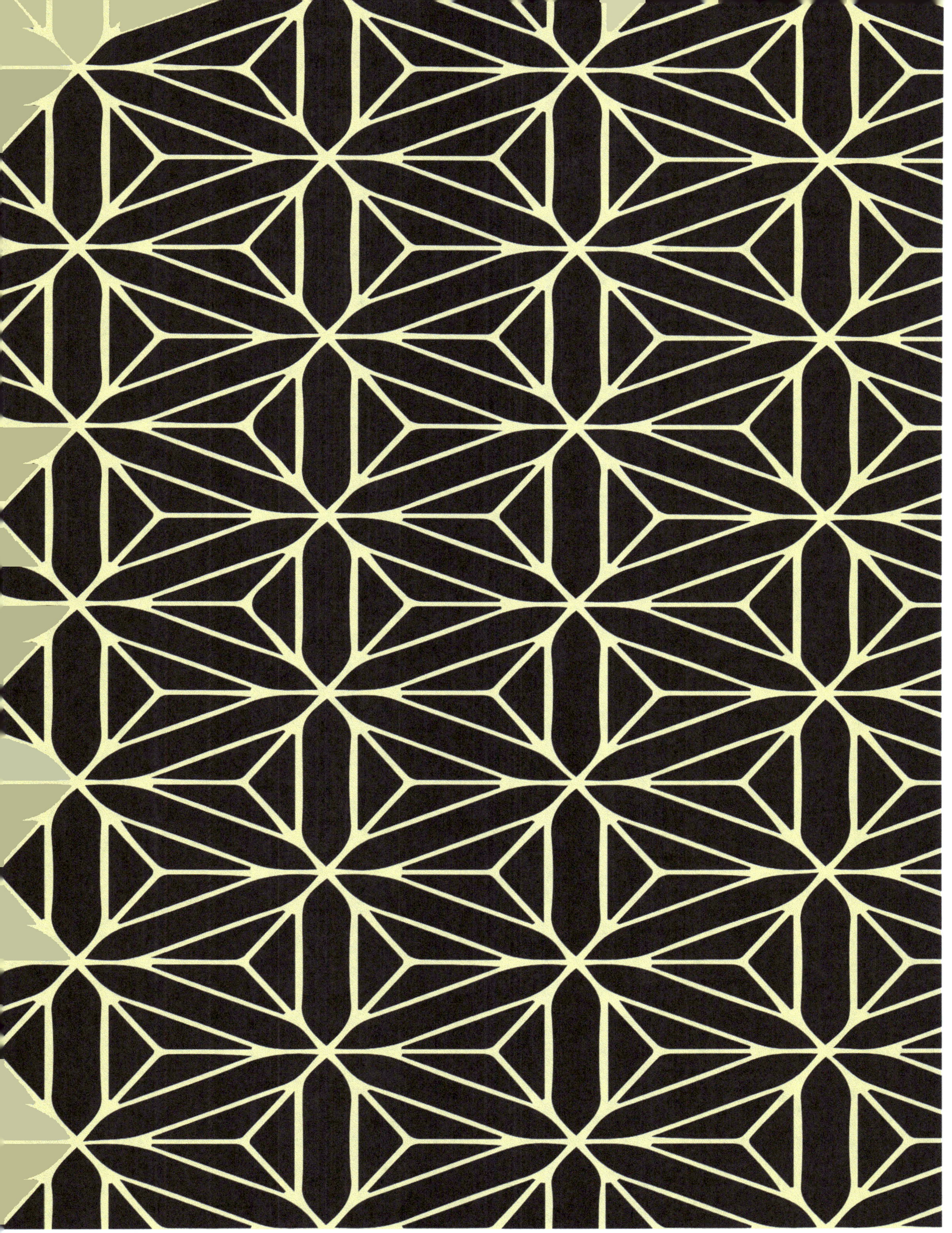

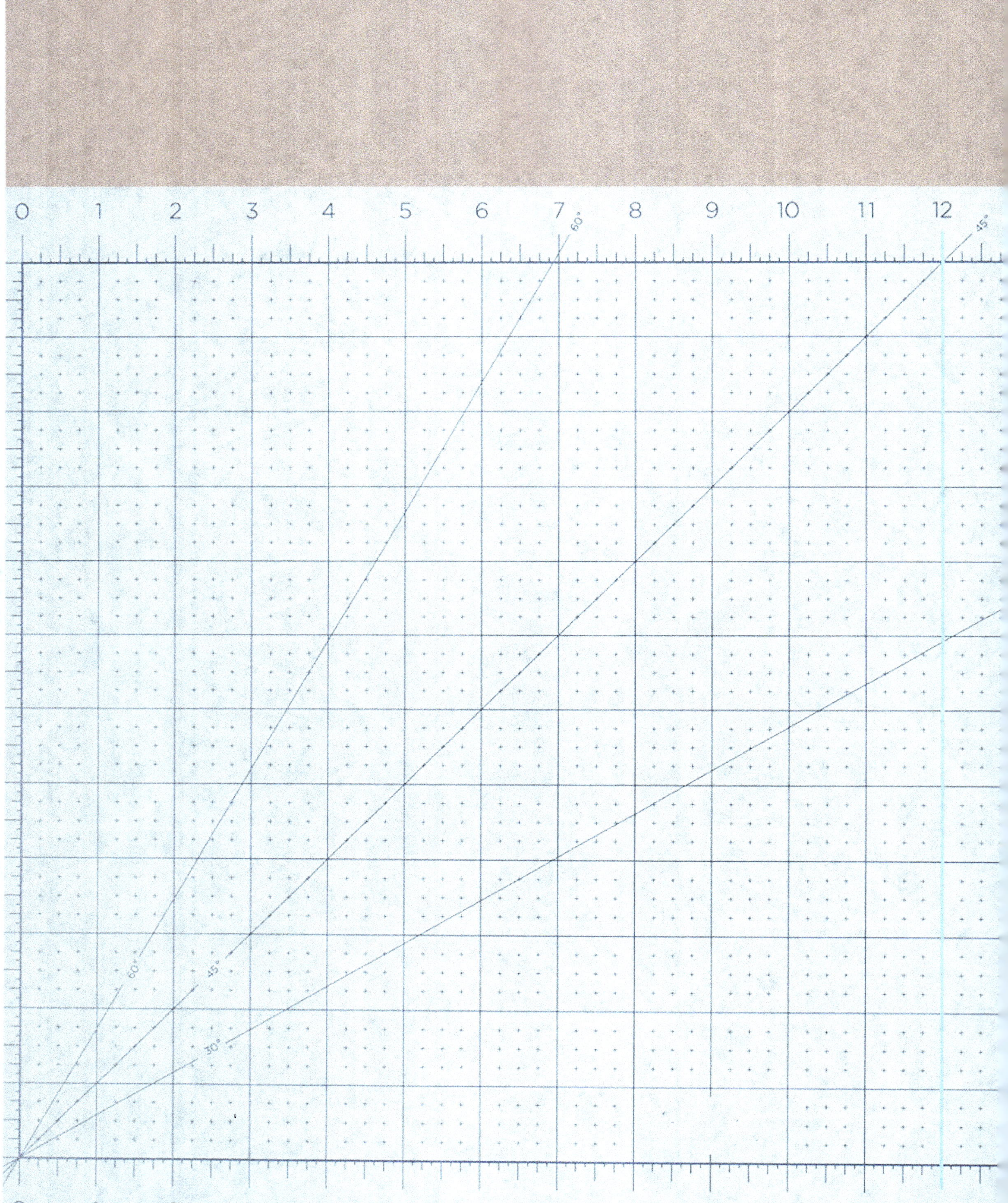

0 1 2 3 4 5 6 7 8 9 10 11 12
60°
45°
60°
45°
30°

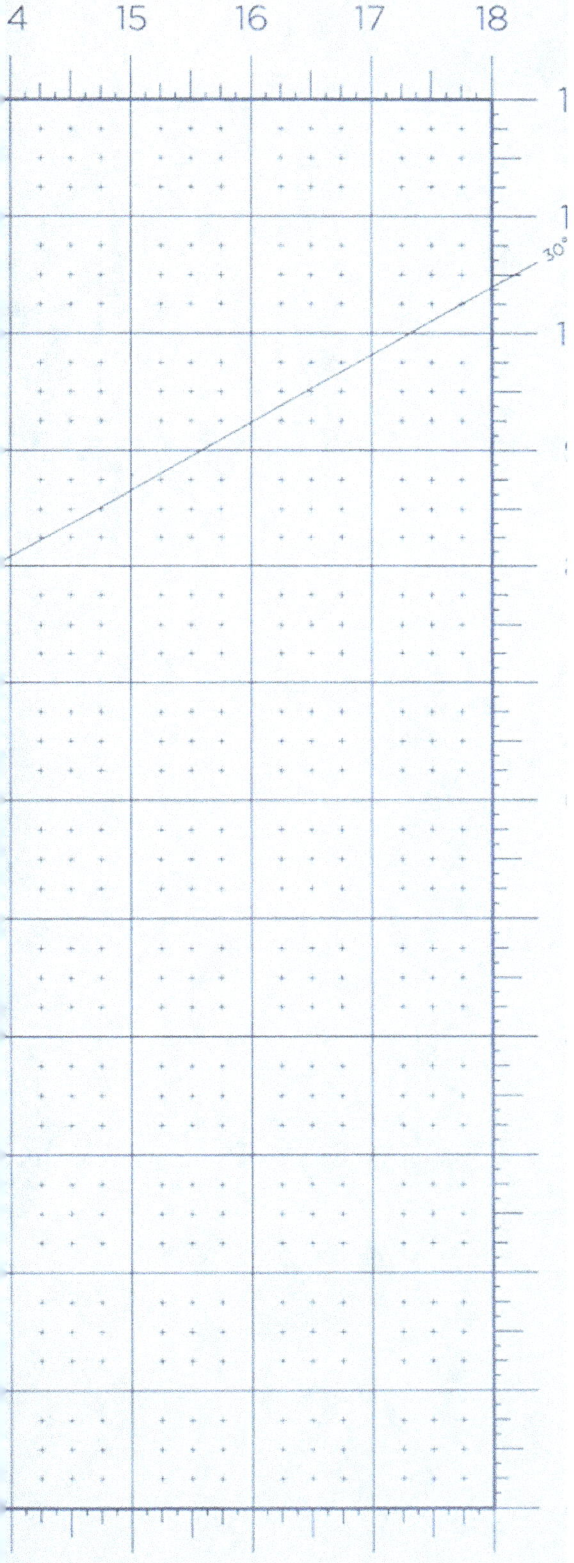

them. You cannot sell or give them away. If a machine is discontinued, your cartridge becomes useless.

Cricut Mat

A Cricut mat is a surface that you will require for cutting out. It provides a foundation on which you create your project.

The materials grip the mat, The level of grips can vary for different mats, and therefore, you may have to change mats for other materials. All the machines come with a Standard Grip mat. You will receive three other mats with Cricut Maker and Explore devices. These mats are light, healthy, and fabric grip.

Cricut Joy comes with two extra mats, which are light and card for cutting out cards. These are compact, just like the machine.

You can purchase more mats according to their quality and grip.

LightGrip mat: With this mat, you can cut paper like construction paper, vellum and regular printer paper, and vinyl.

StandardGrip mat: It lets you cut cardstock, embossed cardstock, vinyl, iron-on, and patterned paper.

FabricGrip mat: It is suitable for fabric and

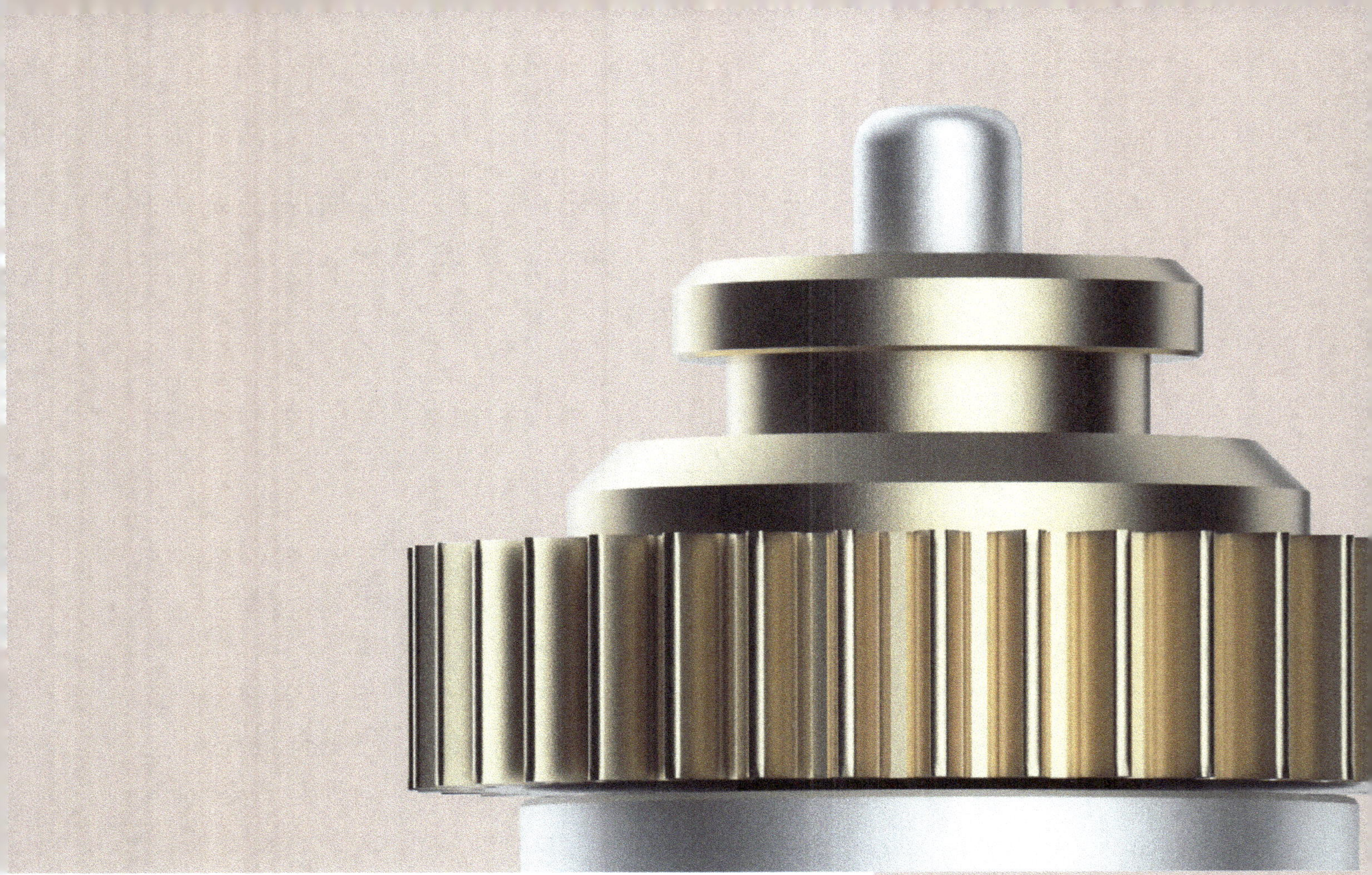

crepe paper.

StrongGrip mat: It is suitable for thicker card-stock, glitter cardstock, stiffened fabric, poster board, chipboard, and magnetic material.

If you are using your mat regularly, take the best care of it to allow it the most extended life. You can care for your carpets in the following ways.

Keep your mat covered when you are not using it to avoid dust and debris sticking on it. Use the basic toolset. Use the scraper to scrape off any excess bits and spatula for removing cuts out of your mat.

Only use recommended material for your mat.

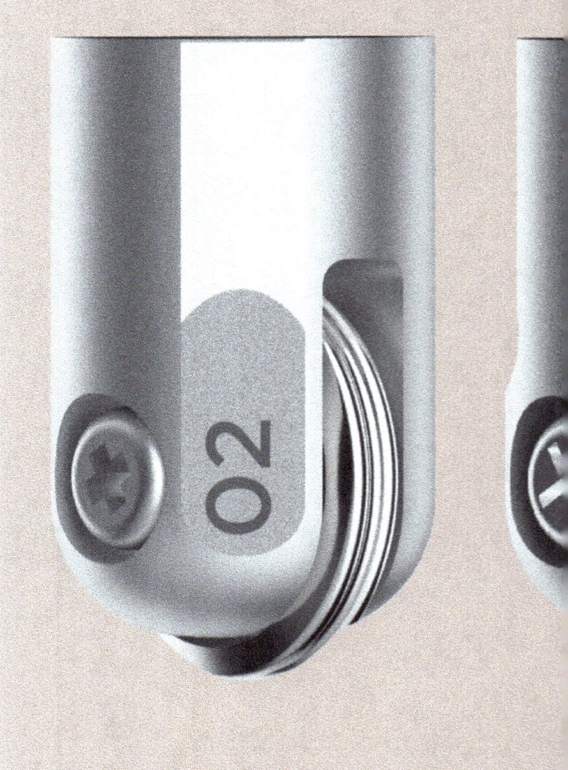

Cricut Blades

Cricut blades are the essential tools that allow all your designs to cut in the machine. Different materials require different blades. Let's understand edges in detail according to the compatible devices.

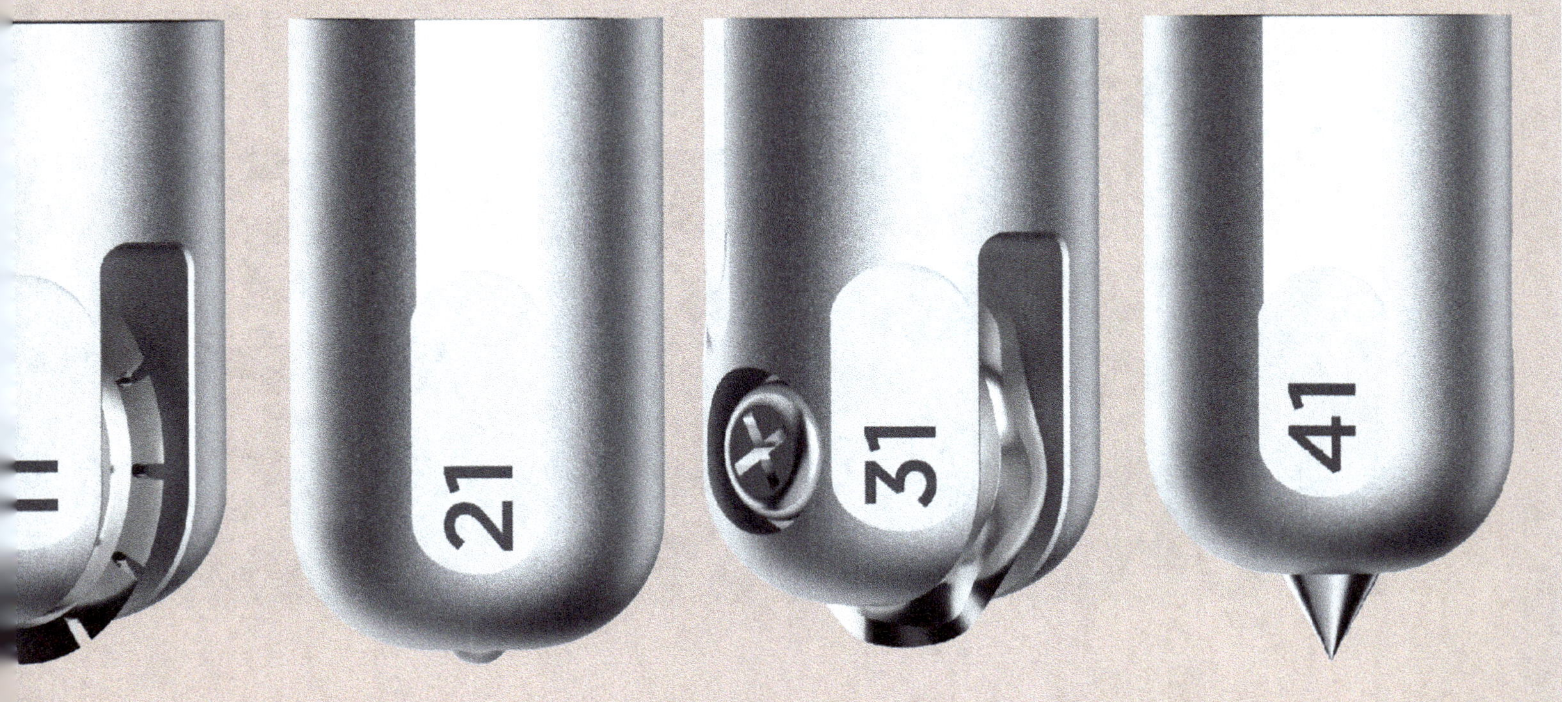

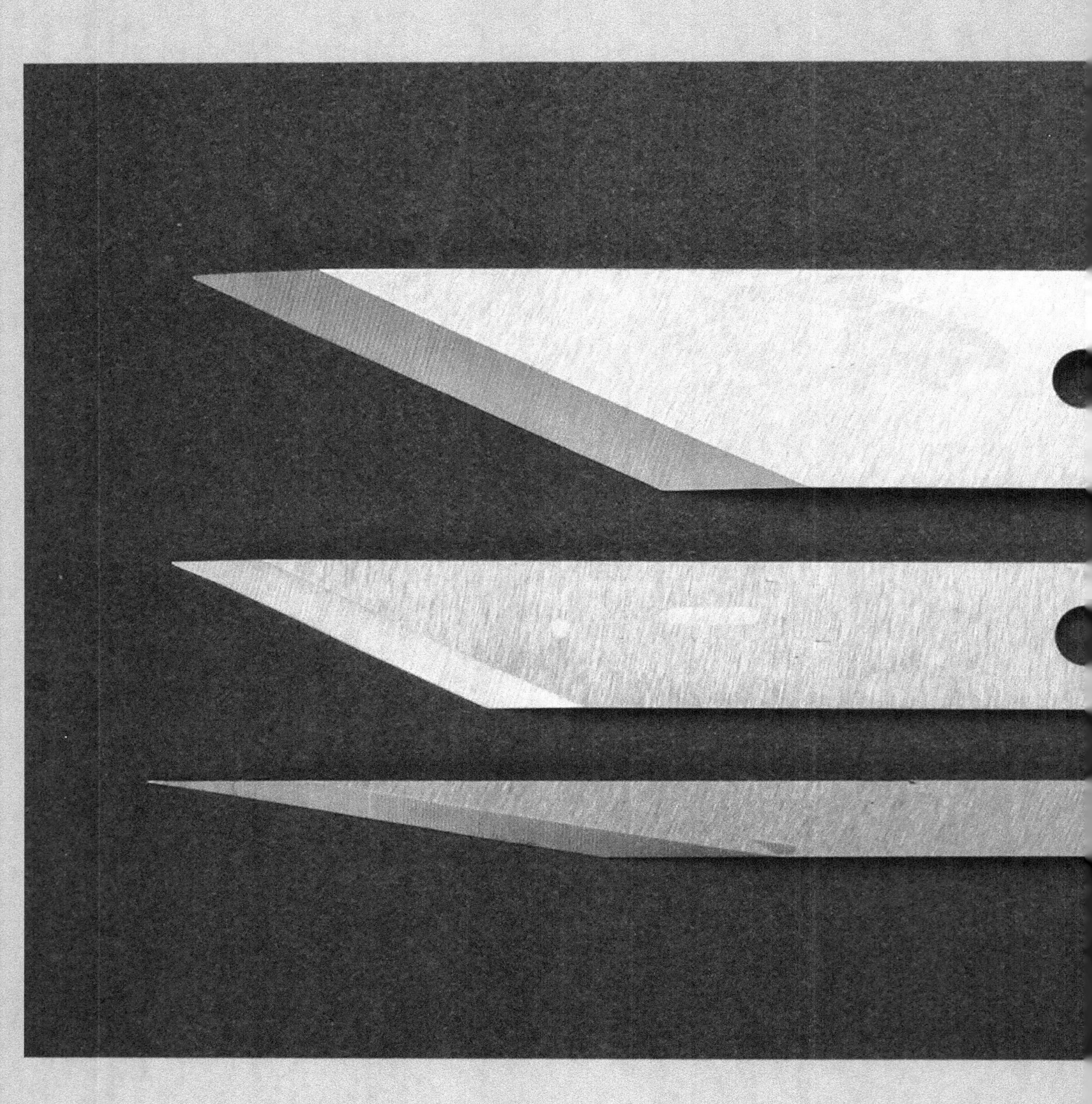

Fine Point Blade

It is the most common blade with all three popular machines, Cricut Joy, Cricut Maker, and Cricut Explore Air 2. It can cut light and medium materials like vinyl, cardstock, canvas, and paper. You can also cut thin faux leather and light chipboards with it.

Deep Point Blade

It works with Cricut Explore Air 2 and Cricut Maker. This blade has a sharper angled edge than the Fine Point Blade. You can cut thicker materials with it, like corrugated paper, aluminum foil, foam, and 0.6 mm thick magnetic sheet and leather.

Bonded Fabric Blade

It works with Cricut Explore Air 2 and Cricut Maker. You can cut fabrics that are bonded to a backing material with this blade. It can cut bonded felt, denim, burlap, oilcloth, polyester, and silk. It is very similar to Fine Point Blade, but it is made for cutting fabric. Do not use it on paper or vinyl, and don't use it if your materials are not bonded; otherwise, it will stretch and rip them and even damage your mat.

Engraving Tip

You can inscribe many flourishes, embellishments, monograms, personalized text, etc., on materials. You can easily mark your favorite quotes on a variety of materials.

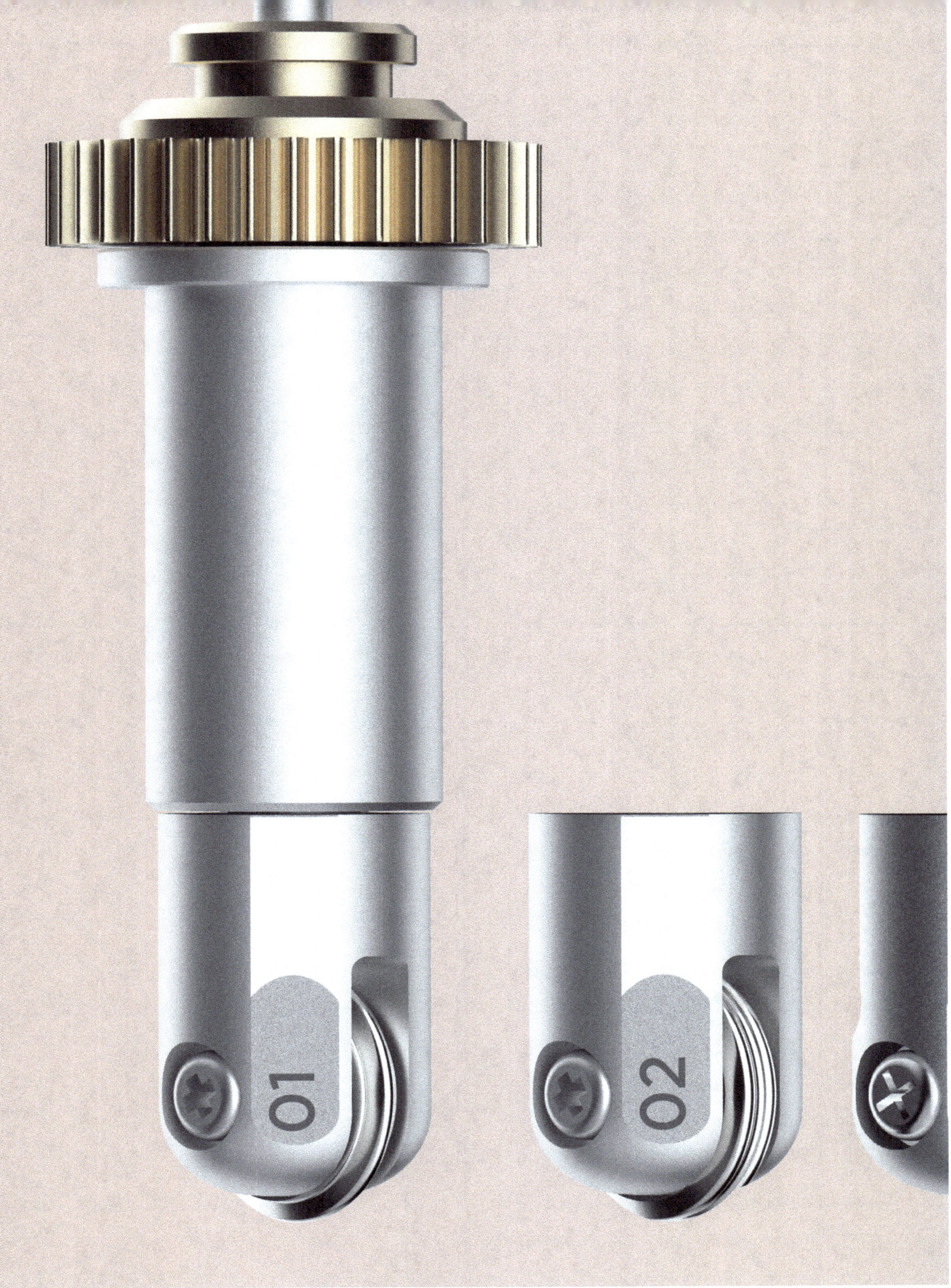

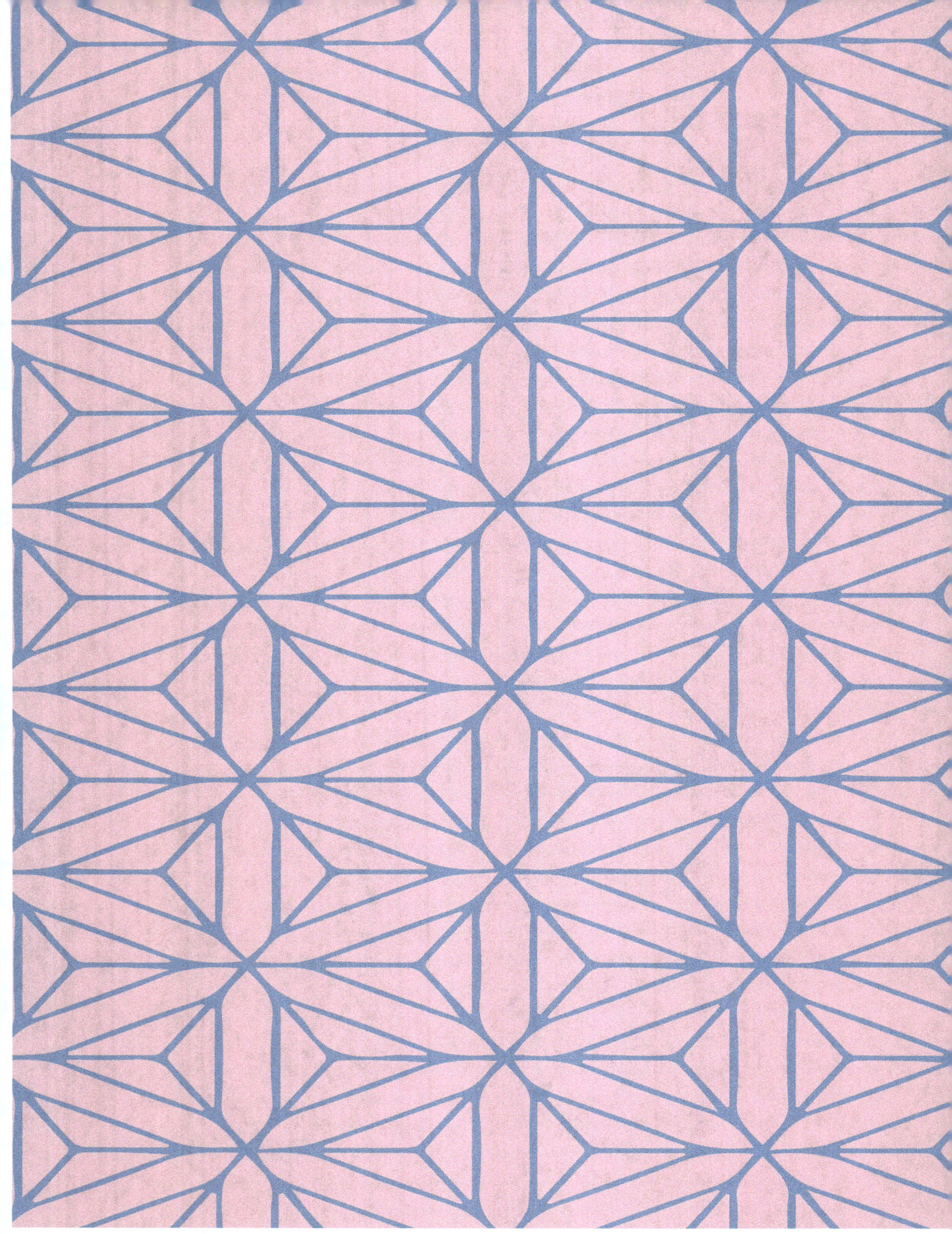

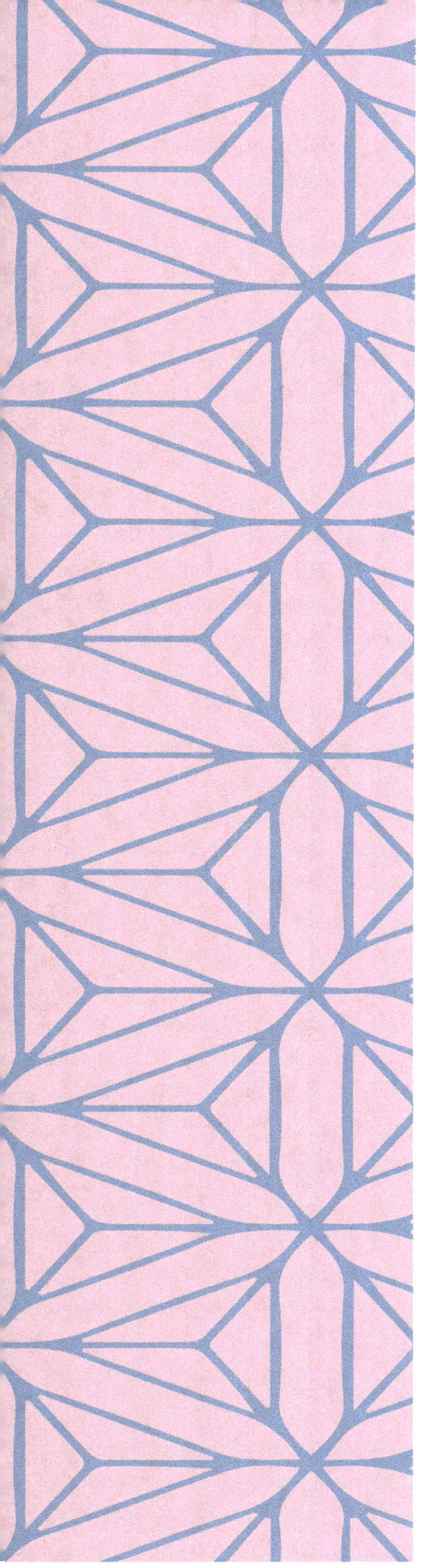

Debossing Tip

You can add specialized polish and eminent elegance to paper crafts with crisp and detailed debossed designs.

Perforation Blade

It can help you to get a perfect tear swiftly and smoothly. You can get precise perforation cuts with a wide variety of projects.

Wavy Blade

A wavy blade helps you to add a fun wavy decorative edge to any design.

Scoring Wheel and Double Scoring Wheel

It gives extra-deep score lines for crisp creases and easy folds on everyday material projects. Changing QuickSwap Tips

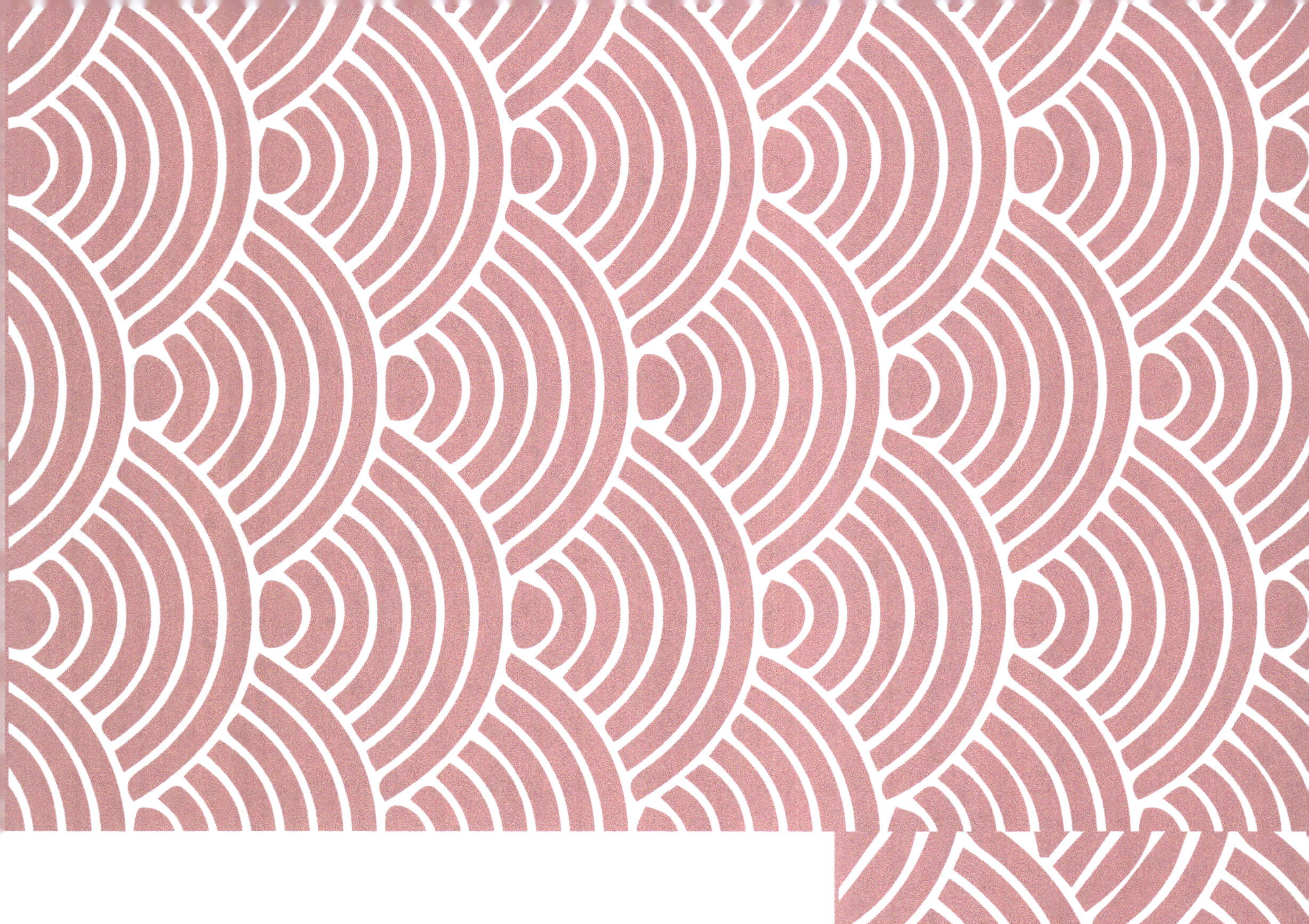

You can swap between debossing, engraving, scoring, and other effects at the touch of a button.

Press and hold a plunger that you will find on the top of QuickSwap Housing. It will release the tip.

Now gently remove the tip.

Keep the plunger pressed, line up flat areas inside new tips with flat sides of the housing, and then slide the information into place. Make sure that the direction is firmly seated against the housing.

Release the plunger to secure the tip in place

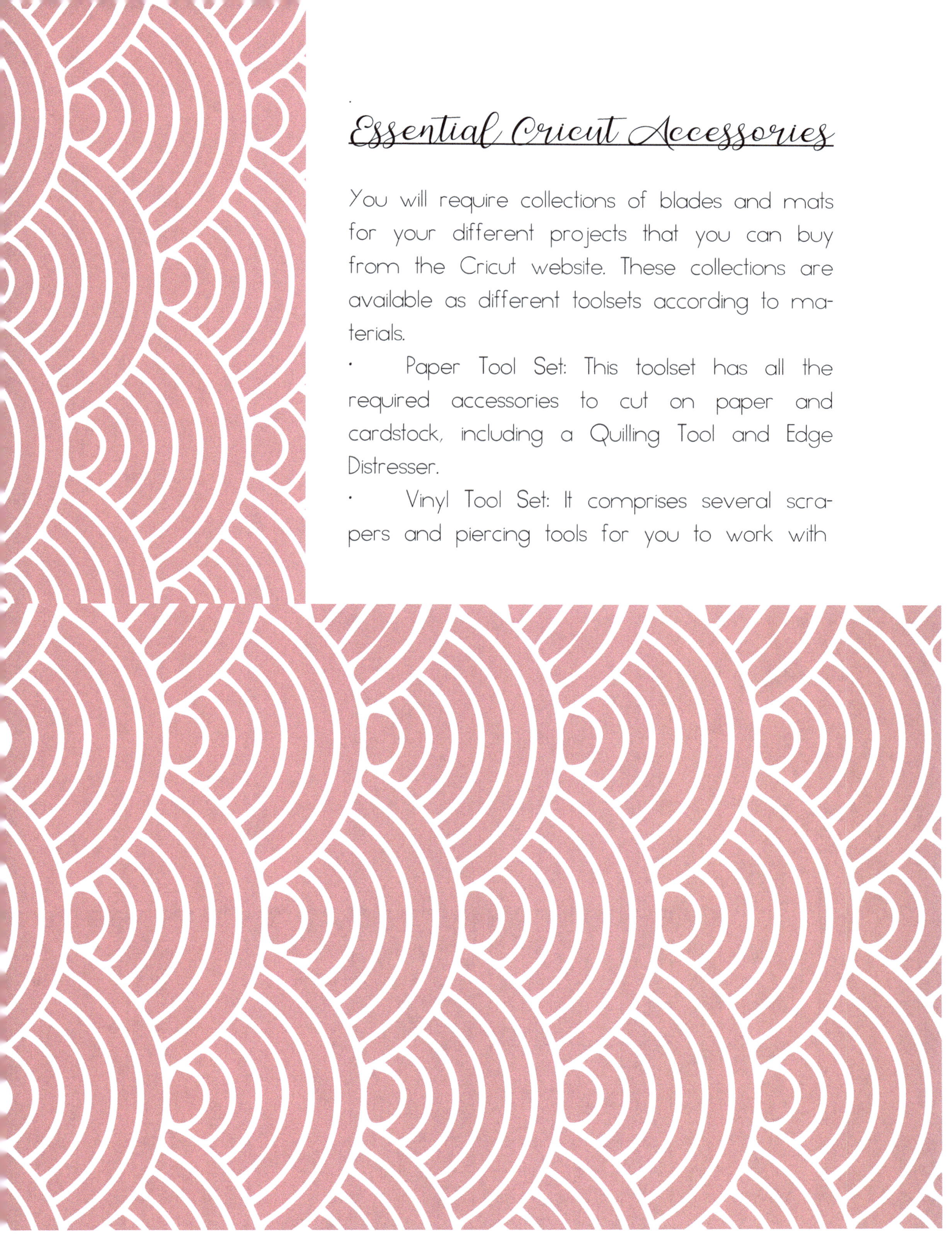

Essential Cricut Accessories

You will require collections of blades and mats for your different projects that you can buy from the Cricut website. These collections are available as different toolsets according to materials.

·   Paper Tool Set: This toolset has all the required accessories to cut on paper and cardstock, including a Quilling Tool and Edge Distresser.

·   Vinyl Tool Set: It comprises several scrapers and piercing tools for you to work with

vinyl.

- Basic Tool Set: It has tools that will help you to keep your project nice and neat. It includes a spatula, weeder, tweezers, etc.
- Essential Tool Set: It comprises the Basic Tool Set and other tools to create scoring lines on your project. You can cut more comprehensive material with its help.

Some Cricut bundles also come with a tool-set. Don't forget to check them out while you are buying your machine.

Cricut BrightPad

It is a work surface having LED light. You can adjust the brightness. If you are working with tiny details with vinyl, fabric, or jewelry, BrightPad can help you a lot.

Infusible Ink

This is a relaxed and beautifully vibrant type of permanent heat transfer. This technology is infusing the ink and the material and is

more significant than iron-on. You can use infusible ink to personalize your T-shirts and other clothing and fabrics to give them a professional look. You can also transfer it to coasters and tote bags.

Infusible Ink is very durable, and therefore it won't go away if you throw your clothes in a washer and dryer. You can also use it with iron-on to create good designs with different textures.

Infusible Ink Transfer Sheets come in different colors as well as pre-designed patterns. You can also use Infusible Ink Pens and Markers to make your transfer sheets. Infusible Ink is stable, so don't worry about spilling it out.

You will require a heat press that can reach a temperature around 400° or 205°C. You can use EasyPress for this purpose.

Here, you will have to be careful regarding the fabrics as cheaper fabrics won't stand the heat required for Infusible Ink. You can use 100 cotton. You cannot use Infusible Ink with Cricut Joy. It only works with Cricut Maker or Cricut Explore Air 2

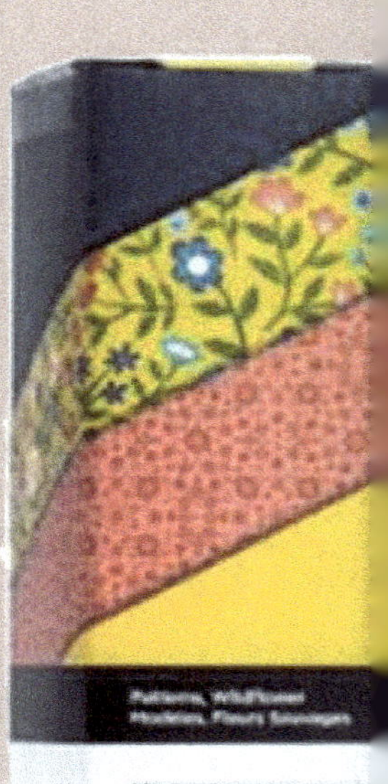
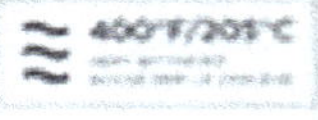

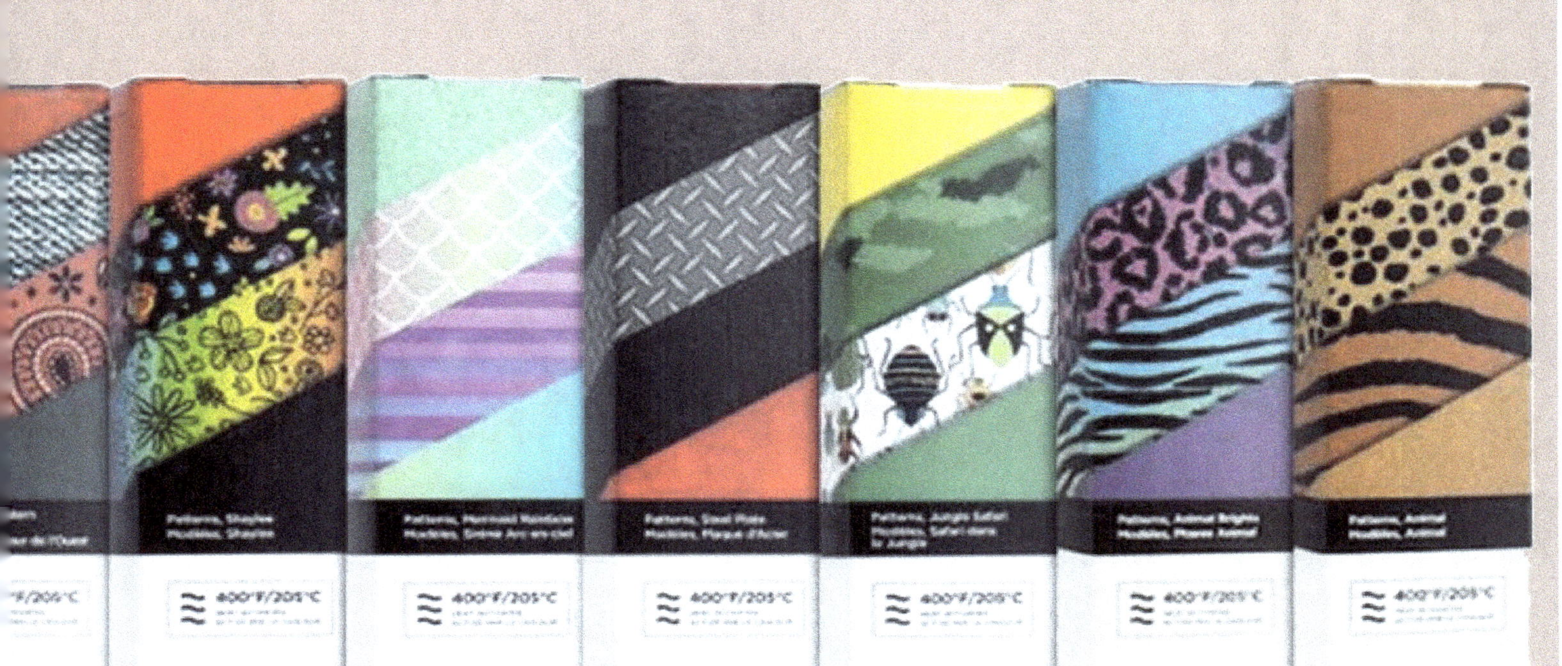

Patterns, Shapes
Modèles, Shapes
Patterns, Mermaid Rainbow
Modèles, Sirène Arc-en-ciel
Patterns, Steel Plate
Modèles, Plaque d'Acier
Patterns, Jungle Safari
Modèles, Safari dans la Jungle
Patterns, Animal Brights
Modèles, Phares Animal
Patterns, Animal
Modèles, Animal
400°F/205°C

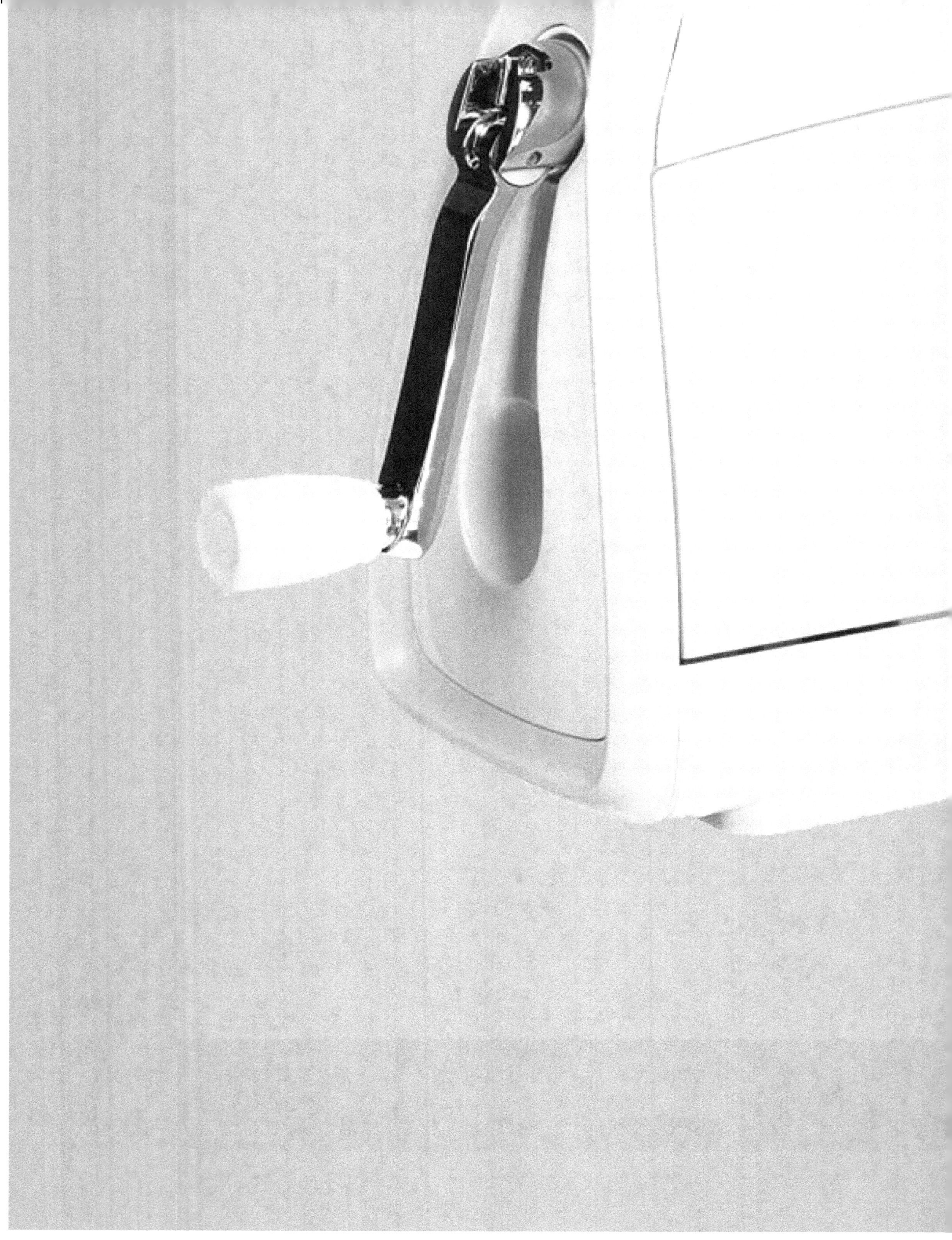

Cricut Cuttlebug

It is a manual machine for die-cutting. It is used for simple cutting and embossing of paper. It is more significant than scissors or knives, but you can't use Design Space features with it. This machine has not been discontinued, but you may get it from other online stores quickly.

Cricut Smart Dial

It is the dial on the top of Cricut Explore Air 2. You can adjust the settings for different materials using this dial which is pre-programmed. You won't have to adjust pressure and other things for standard materials.

These preloaded material settings are for vinyl, poster board, cardstock, fabric, light cardstock, paper, and iron-on. You can also apply your custom setting, which you can choose from pre-set material settings in Design Space.

Cricut SnapMat

SnapMat feature is for your iPhone and only works with iOS. You can picture your material on the cutting mat with its help and see a virtual preview in Design Space. It helps you to see if your designs are placed perfectly or not. It only works with Cricut Maker and Cricut Explore Air 2.

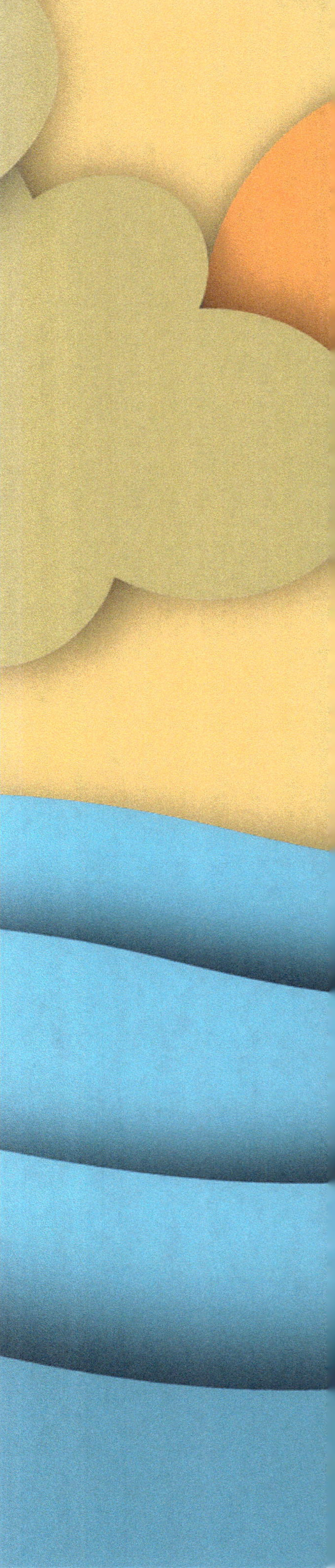

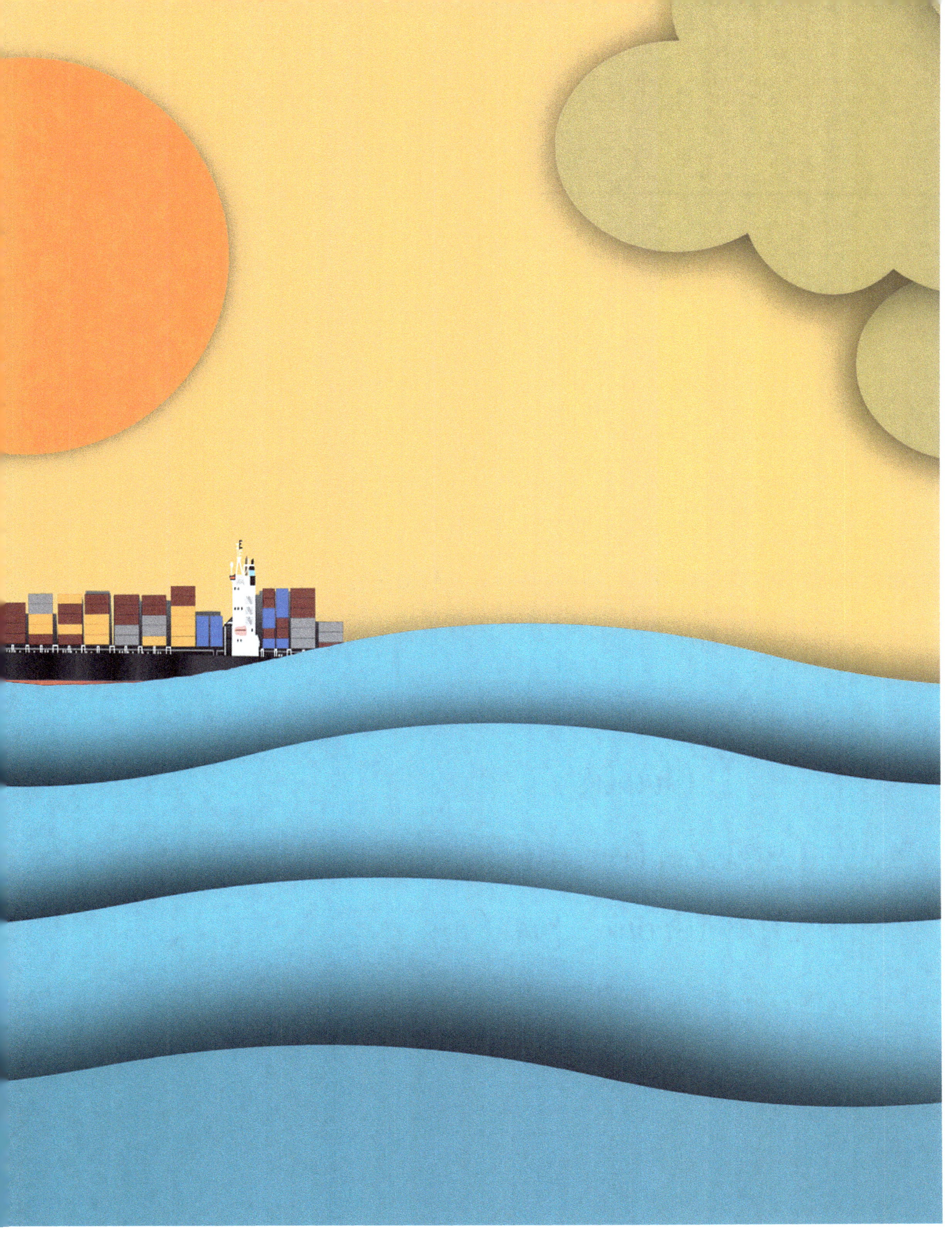

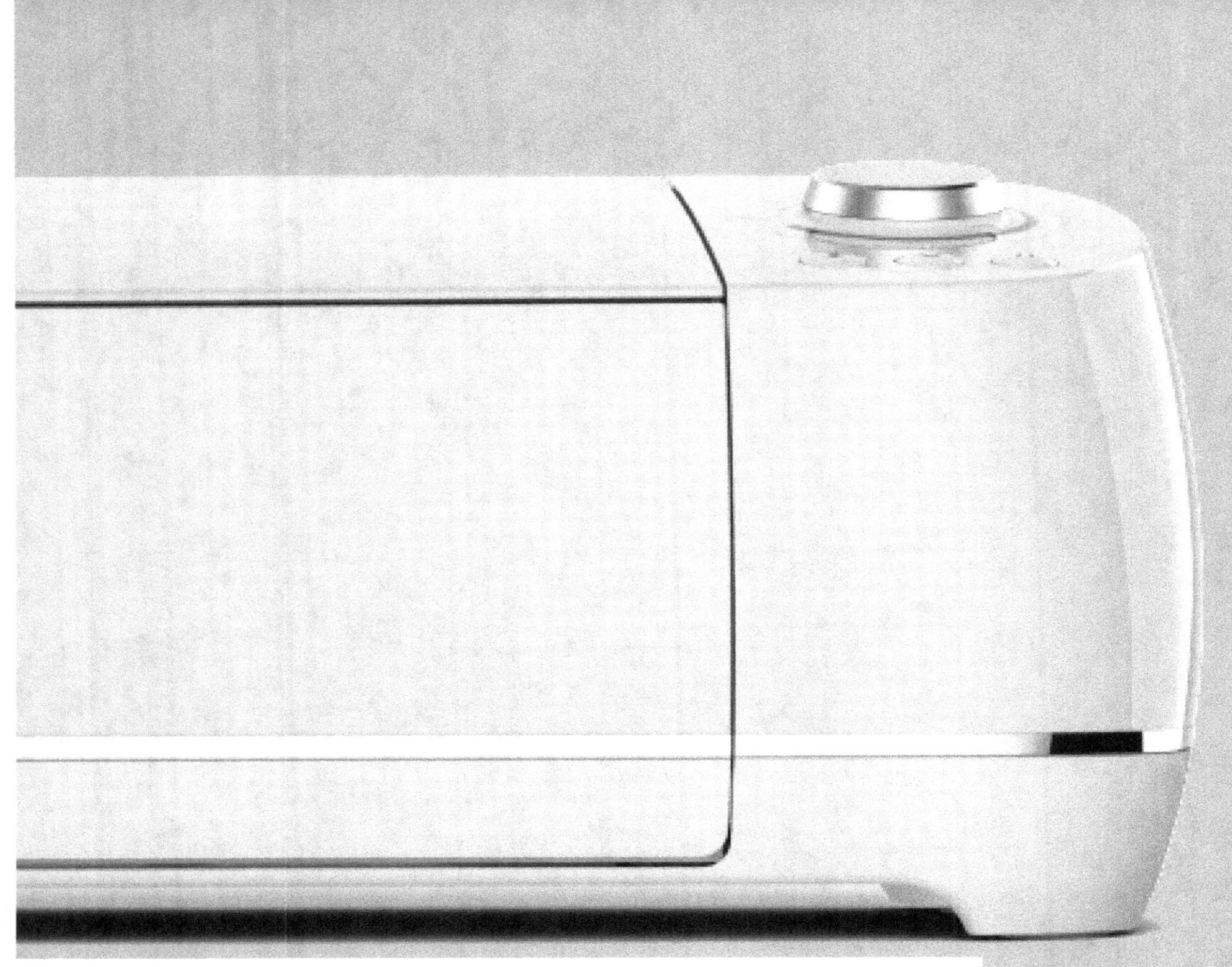

Chapter 7
Cricut Explore Air 2 Tools Maintenance And Care

Changing Cutting Machine Blades

At times, the cutting blades will become blunt, especially with continuous use. There are replacement blades that can be purchased to maintain precise precision cuts.

These blades are sold separately from the blade housing compartments and are not difficult to change. Although care should always be taken as the edges may be blunt for cutting, they will still be considered sharp and cut through the skin.

For Cricut cutting machine blades that use blade housings like the Bonded-Fabric blade and

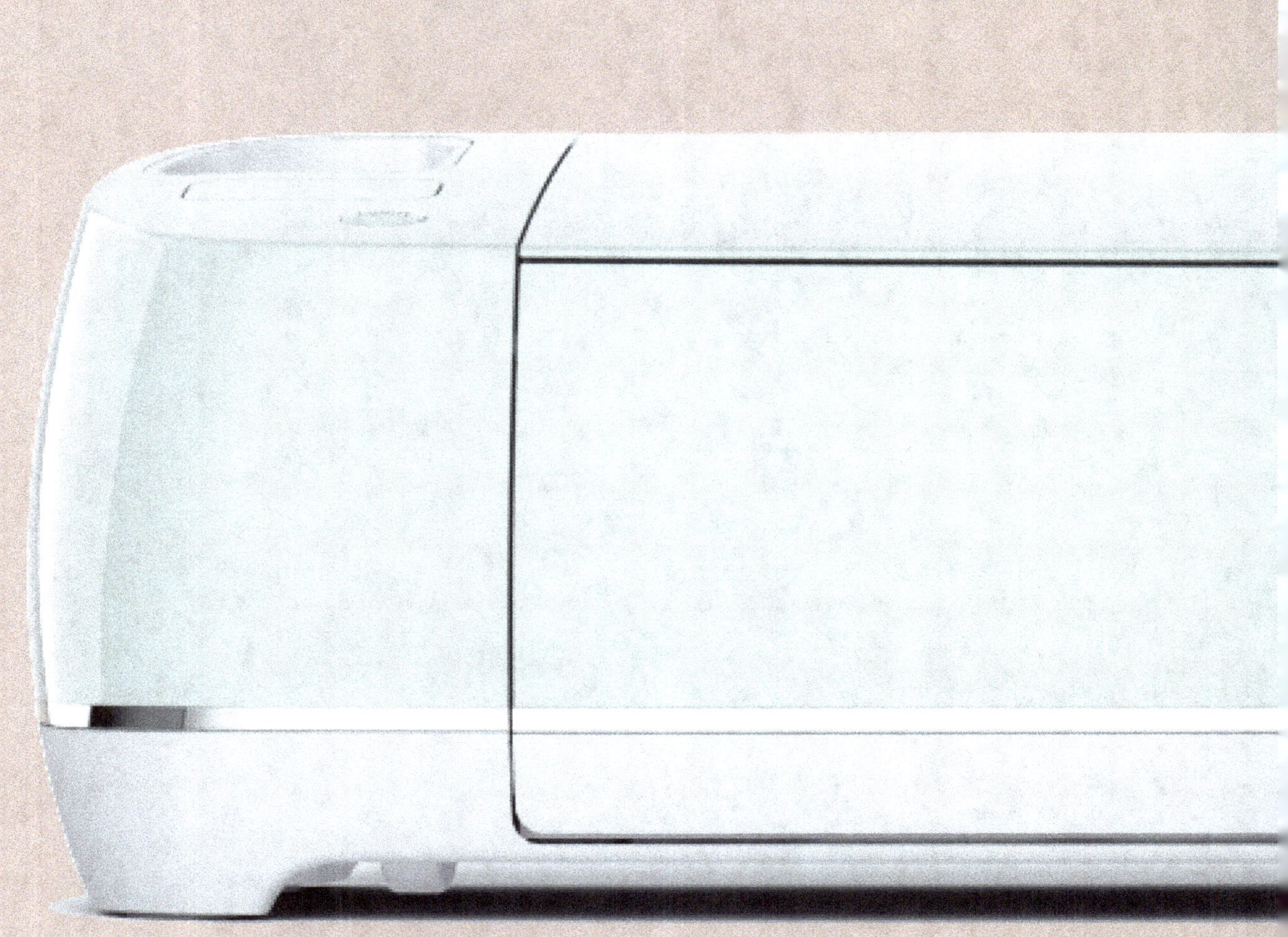

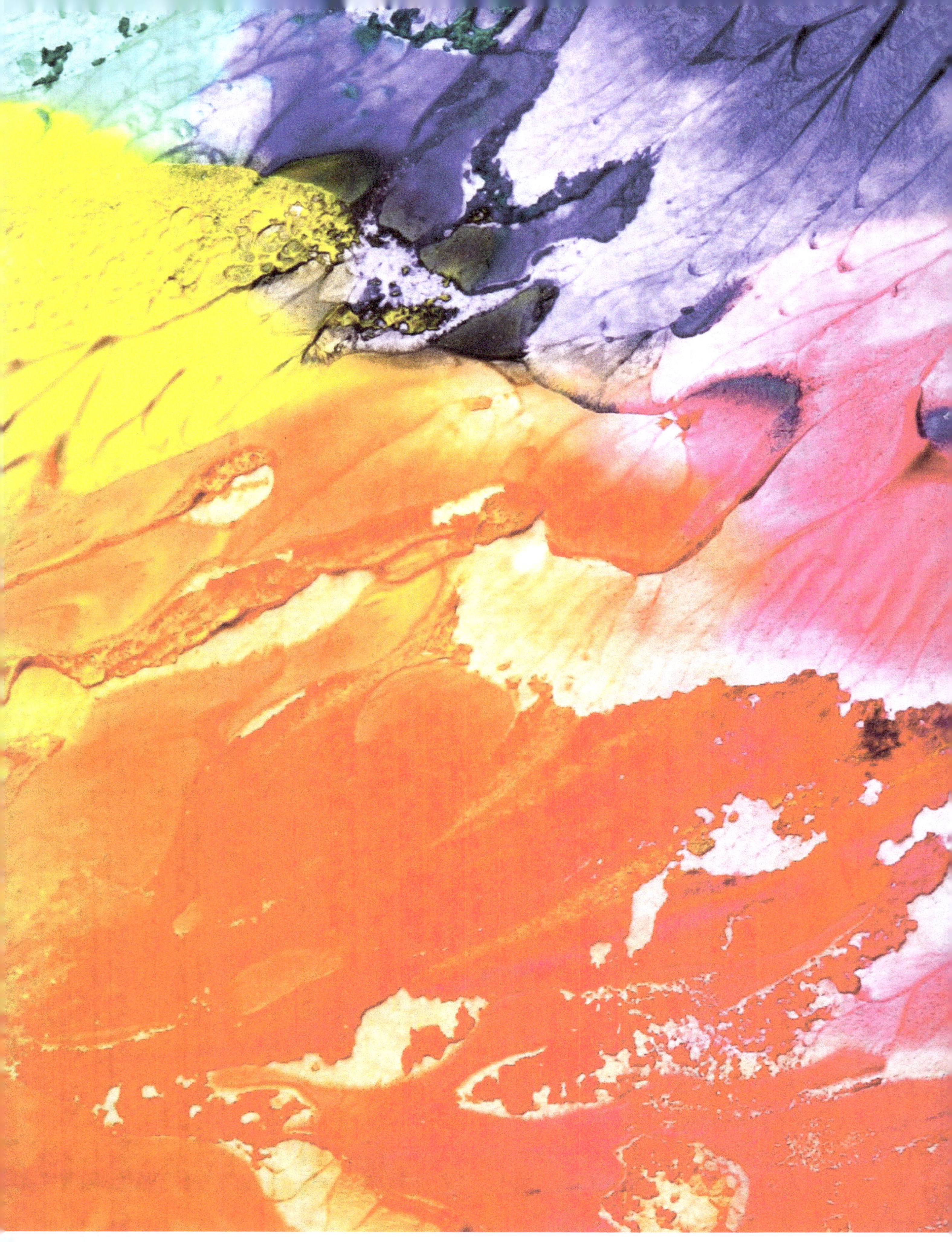

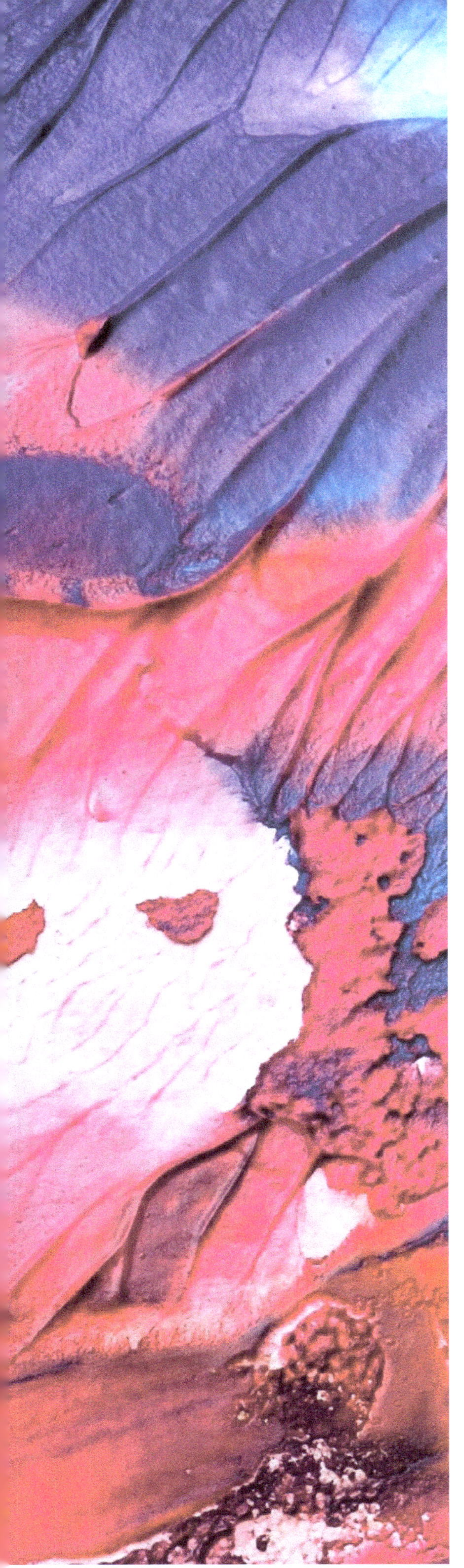

the Fine Point blade:

·	Press down on the dope of the blade housing cap.

·	Pull out the blade (be careful as it can still cut).

·	Hold the housing with the blade side up.

·	Slide the new blade into position until it clicks.

·	Cricut cutting machine blades that use the gear housing (housing with the gold gear on top) utilize blades like the Rotary blade or the Scoring blade:

·	Like the scoring blade and the rotary blade, these blades are a little more complicated and require more assembly.

·	The new blades come with a blade kit:

·	The kit comes with an empty cap that contains the new blade and washer.

·	The kit also comes with a small screwdriver.

·	Each blade comes with a protective cap. Place the protective cap over the blade housing.

·	You will note that the small screw at the bottom of the blade is accessible through the protective cap.

·	Use the small screwdriver to unscrew this little screw and put the little screw to one side.

·   Pull the cap with the bottom blade off of the drive blade housing.

·   Place the blade housing into the new protective cap that contains the new blade and washer.

·   Push the cap on tight and make sure that the screw holes line up.

·   Using the little screw that you took out of the old blade, screw it into the new edge using the tiny screwdriver until it is securely positioned.

Caring for Cricut Cutting Blades

If you want to extend your Cricut cutting machine blades' life, you will need to take care of them.

-       Always make sure that you only use the blades for the materials that they are compatible with. Trying to use the edges on materials too tough for them will blunt if not break the blade.

-       Most blades come with a protective cap. When these blades are not

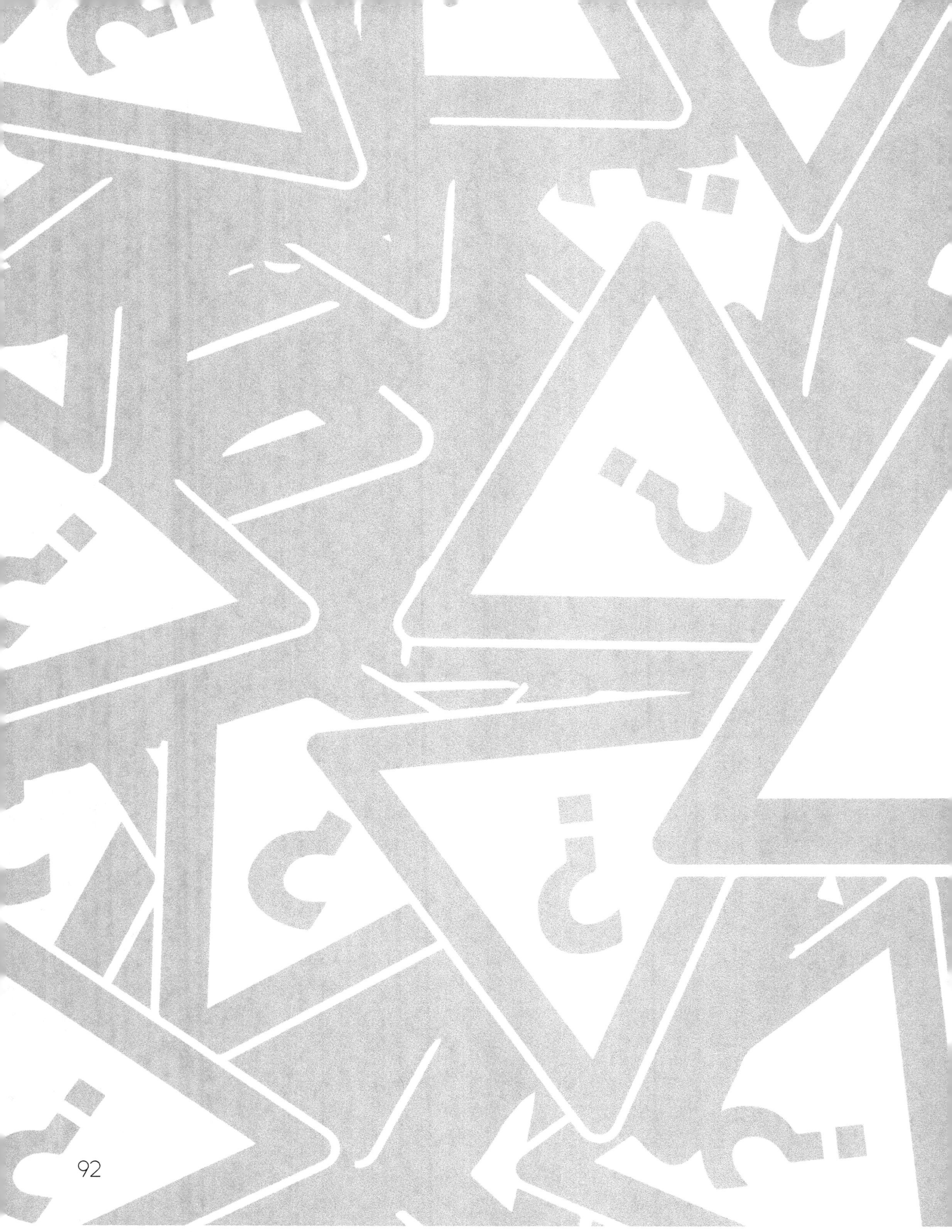

in use, store them safely with their protective covers firmly in place.

-        Make sure that you store them in a place that is free of dust and grime. The best site is in the Cricut's storage drawer, as these close away and protect the blades from dust and dirt.

-        To sharpen the blades, you can use a piece of crumpled-up aluminum foil and poke holes in it with the edge for two to three minutes. But this is not ideal, and a blunt blade should be replaced to maintain the cutting machine's precision cutting ability.

Cleaning and Maintaining the Cutting Mats

The Cricut cutting mats are sticky to keep materials being cut firmly anchored to the mat during cutting. These mats can become clogged with particles, especially carpets used with the new Knife Blade that works with the Cricut Maker.

To clean the mats:

·   Never try to scrape any leftover material from the mat. This can damage the carpet and will remove its stickiness.

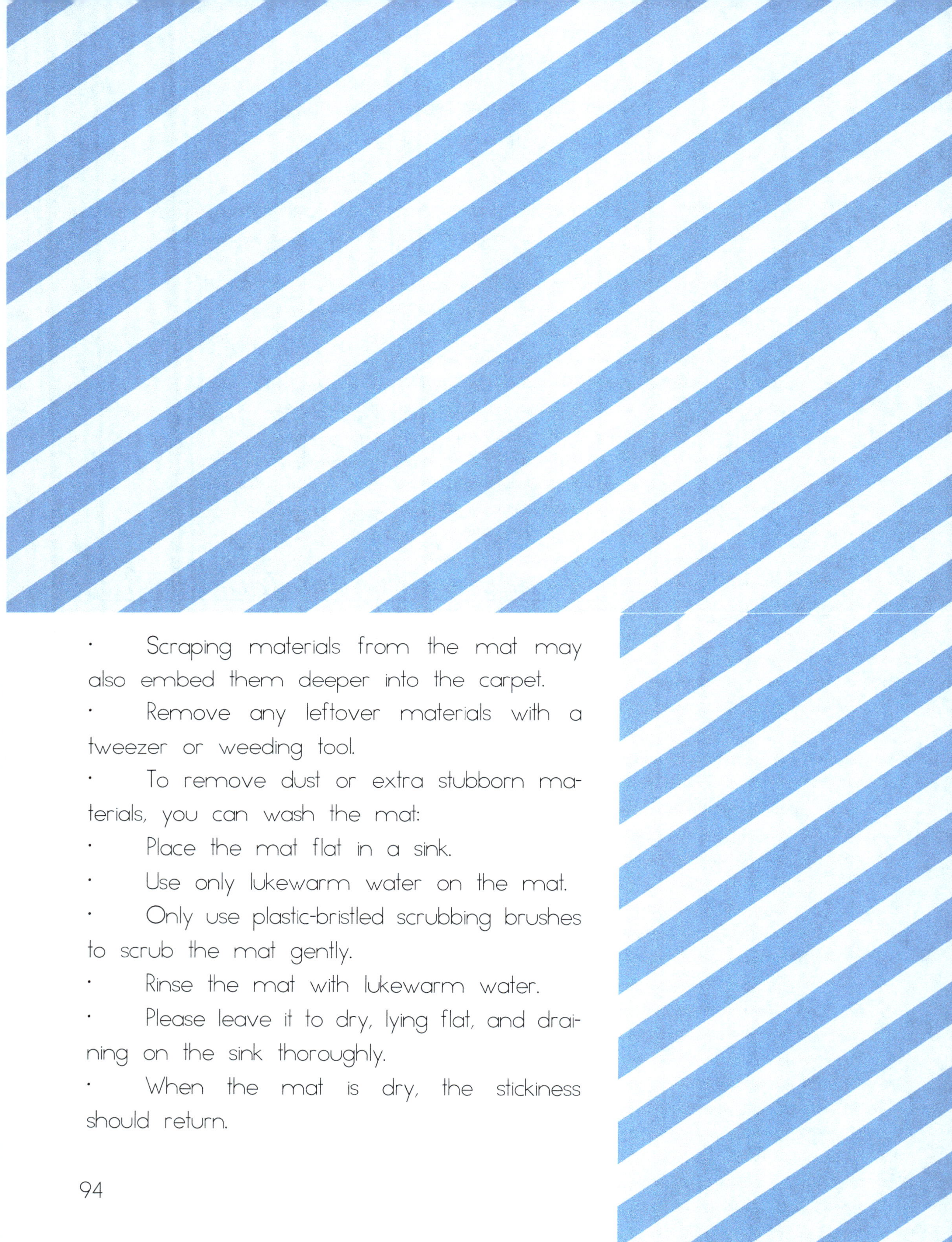

- Scraping materials from the mat may also embed them deeper into the carpet.
- Remove any leftover materials with a tweezer or weeding tool.
- To remove dust or extra stubborn materials, you can wash the mat:
- Place the mat flat in a sink.
- Use only lukewarm water on the mat.
- Only use plastic-bristled scrubbing brushes to scrub the mat gently.
- Rinse the mat with lukewarm water.
- Please leave it to dry, lying flat, and draining on the sink thoroughly.
- When the mat is dry, the stickiness should return.

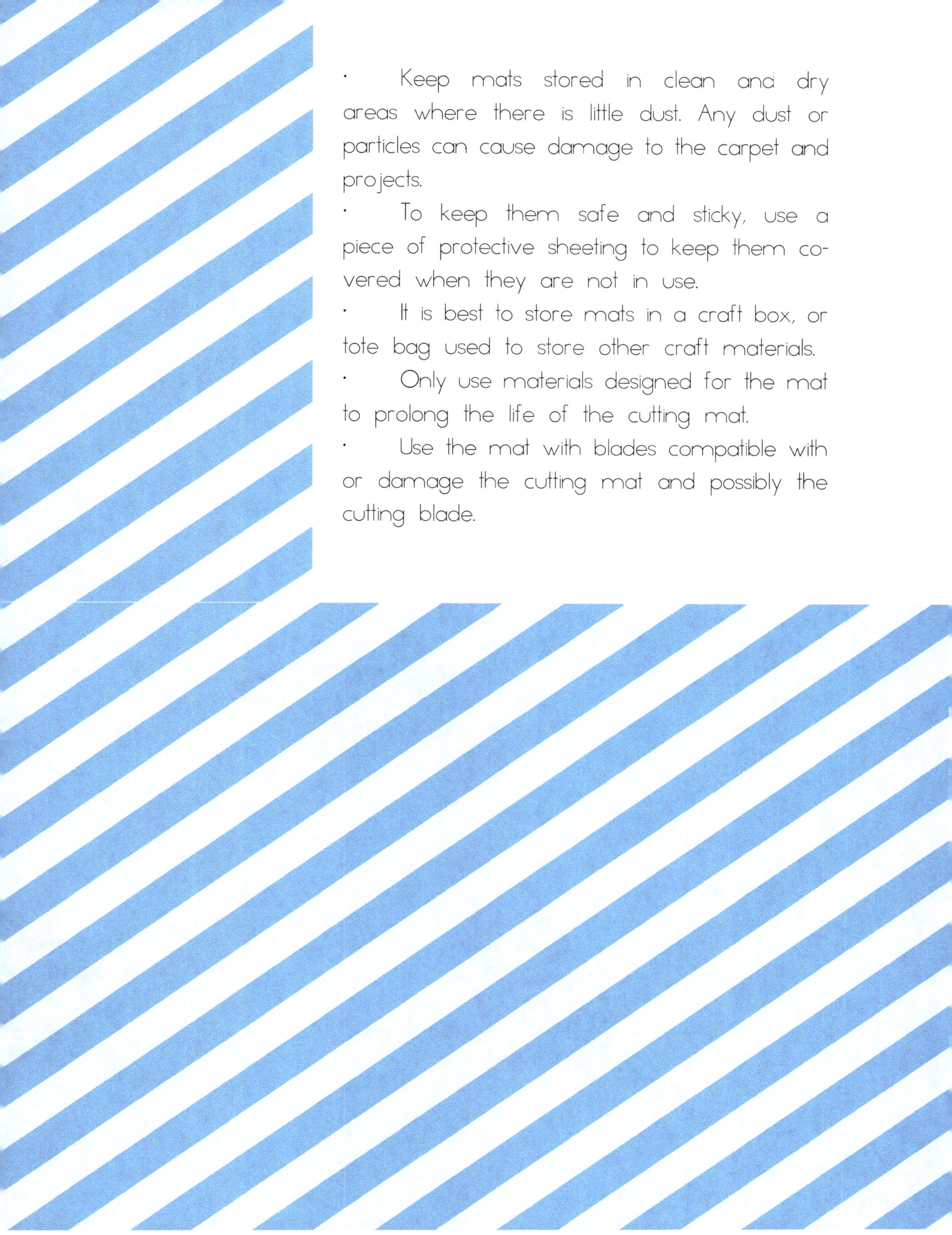

- Keep mats stored in clean and dry areas where there is little dust. Any dust or particles can cause damage to the carpet and projects.
- To keep them safe and sticky, use a piece of protective sheeting to keep them covered when they are not in use.
- It is best to store mats in a craft box, or tote bag used to store other craft materials.
- Only use materials designed for the mat to prolong the life of the cutting mat.
- Use the mat with blades compatible with or damage the cutting mat and possibly the cutting blade.

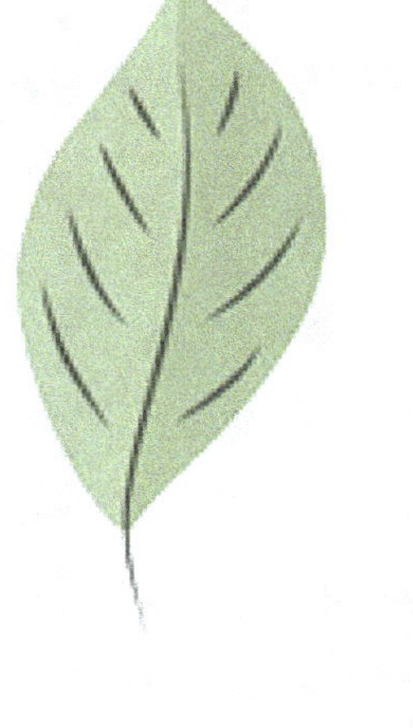

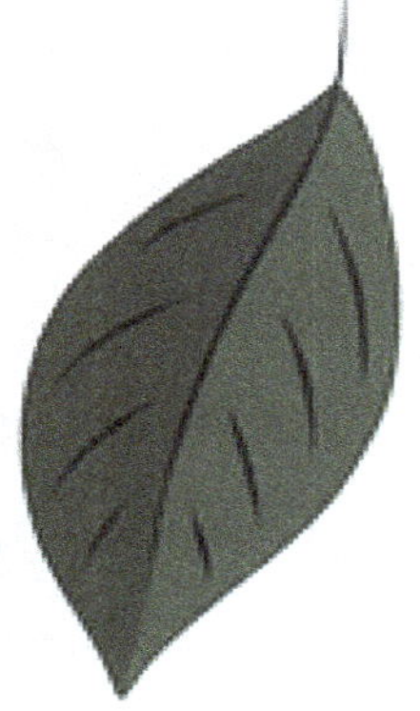

Cleaning the Cricut Cutting Machine

The Cricut machine will get dirty as it cuts paper, cardboard, vinyl and is exposed to everyday dust. The device is not difficult to clean either; all you need is a soft cloth and some glass cleaner spray.

Here are some cleaning tips:

- Never use anything that is corrosive or can damage the machine to clean it. Stay away from acetone (nail polish remover), strong cleaners that contain harsh ingredients such as bleach, or strong countertop cleaners.

- Always make sure that the machine is turned off and unplugged before attempting to clean it.

- If there is grease buildup on the rollers or dirt on any of the feeder bars or roller wheels, use a cotton puff with some window cleaner on it.

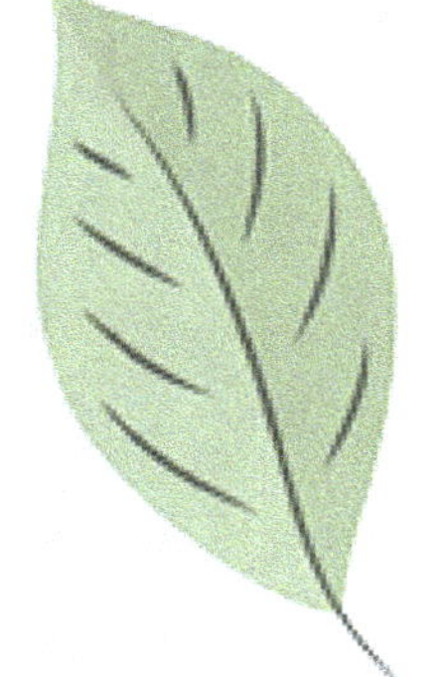

Caring for the Machine, Accessories, and Tools

The best way to care for the machines, accessories, and tools for the Cricut machines is to keep them safely stored away when they are not in use.

Most of the accessories and tools can fit into the Cricut's storage drawers (for the machines that have storage compartments, that is). It is advisable for the devices that do not buy one of Cricut's amazing storage totes.

Keep the tools clean by wiping them off before they are stored and after being used. You can even run them under lukewarm water, pat them dry, and let them drain before you keep them.

Caring for the Cut Smart Carriage in the Cricut Cutting Machine

The little carriage that houses the cutting blades and accessories is called the Cut Smart Carriage.

From time to time, you may notice it getting a little stuck or not moving freely. This may mean that there is a little dust or goo on it, or it may need a little bit

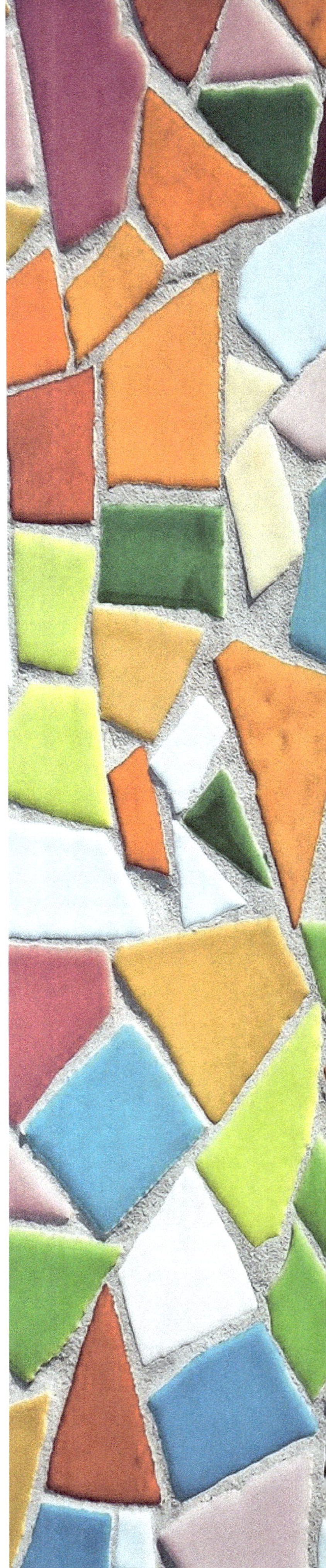

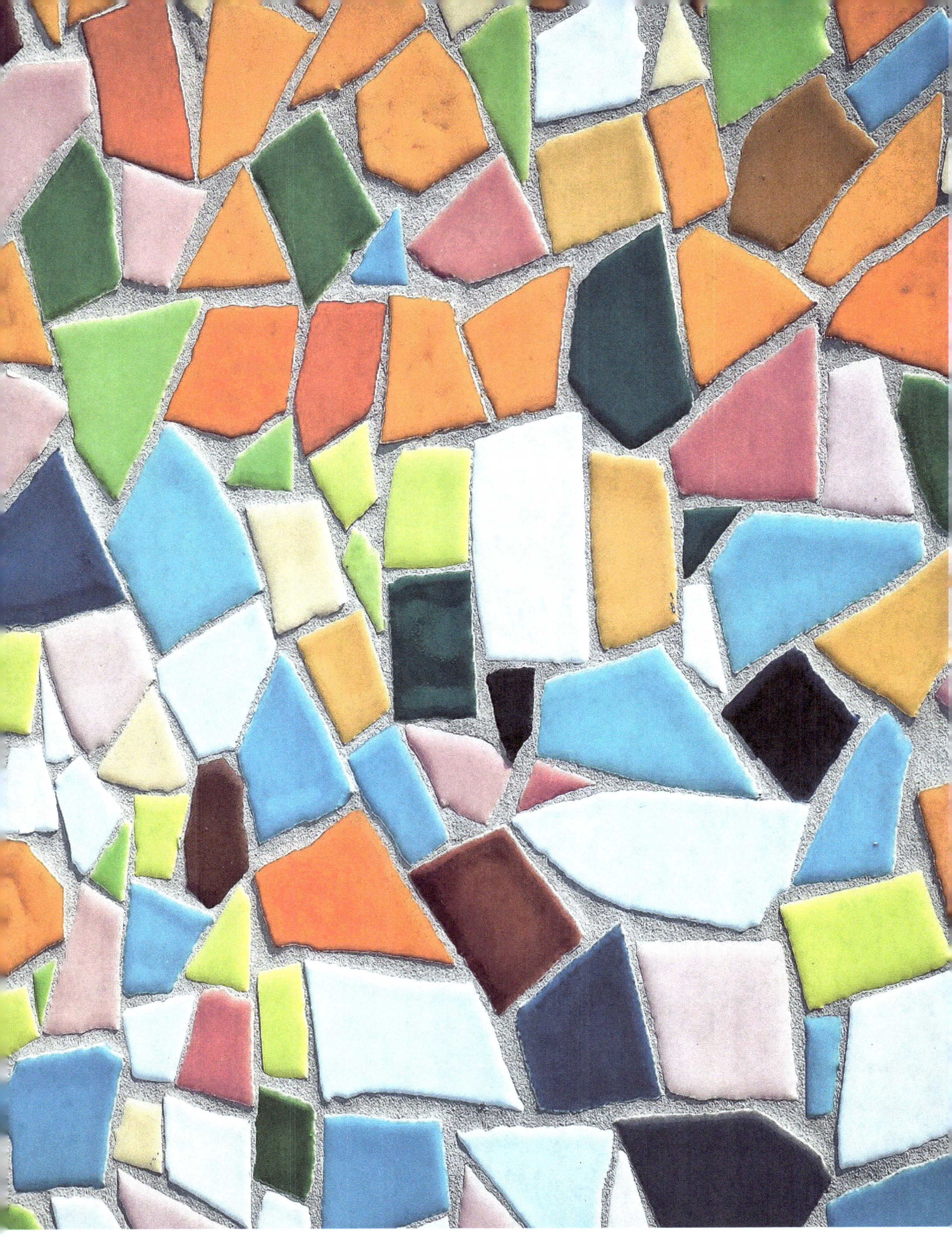

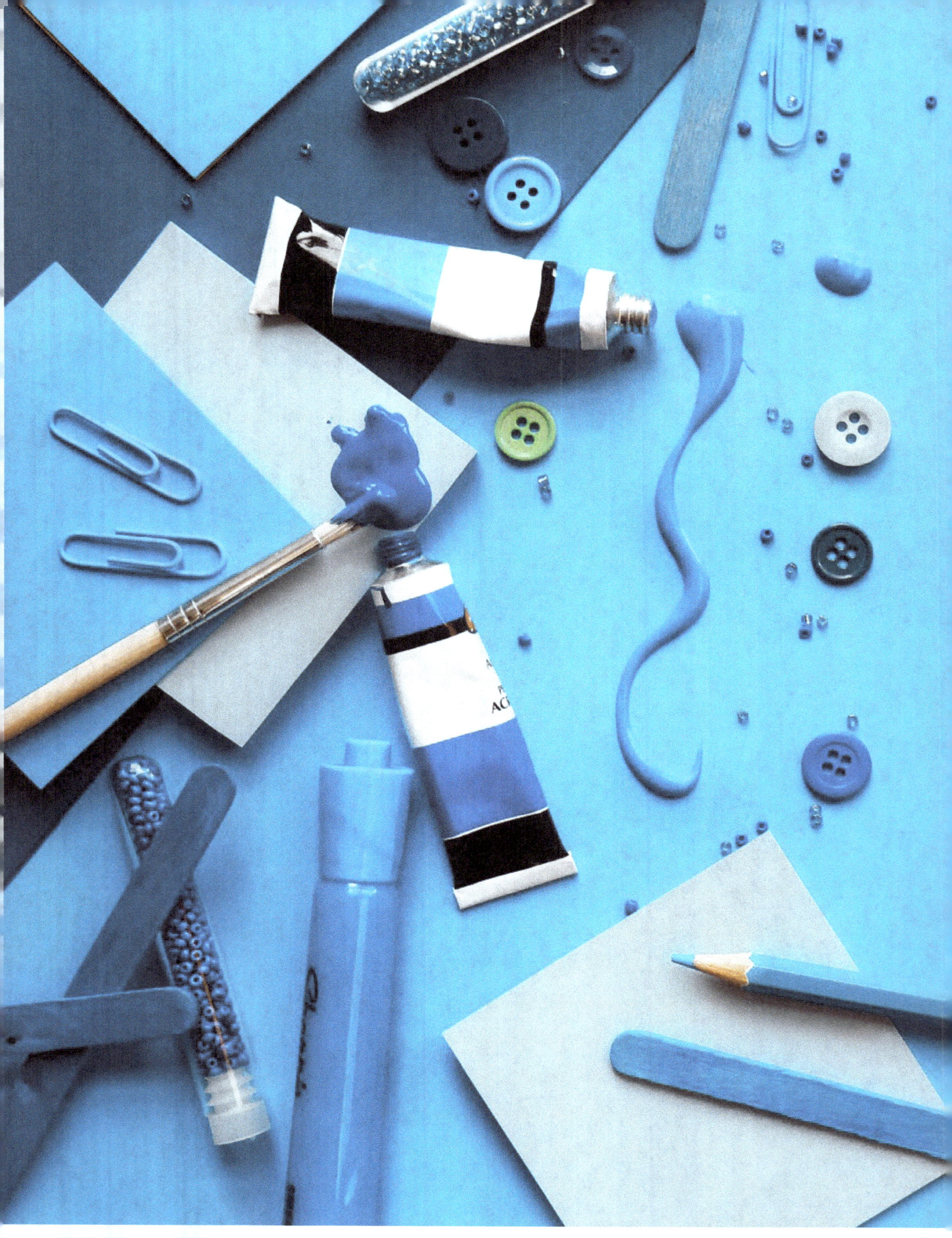

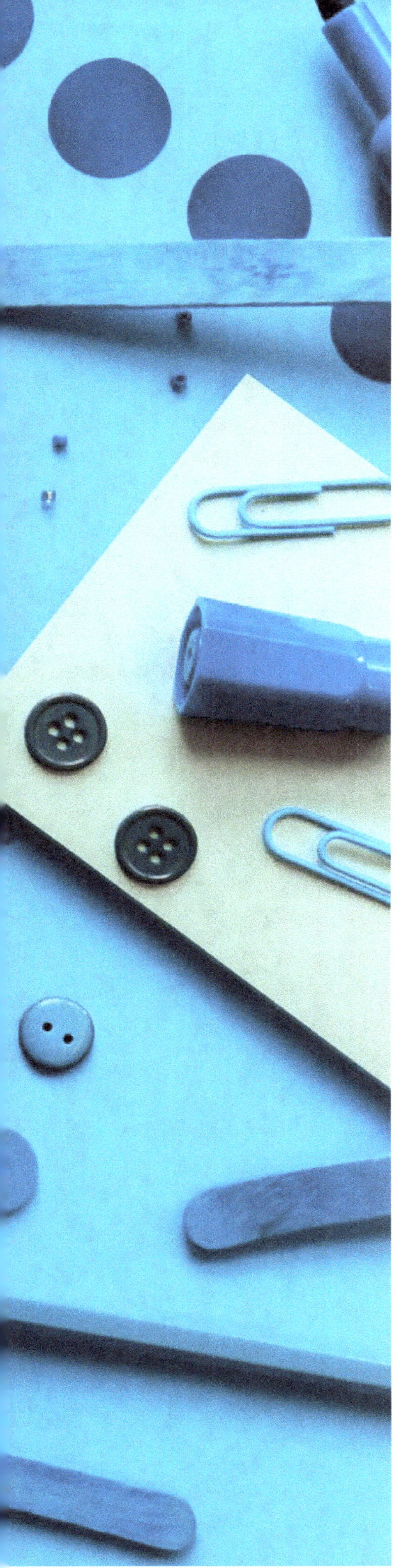

of grease.

Here are some tips on cleaning and greasing the Cut Smart Carriage:

-       Ensure that the cutting machine is turned off and unplugged from the wall before you attempt to clean the carriage.

-       To get the carriage to move to the side to clean it, simply push it to the side. Do not force it, be gentle.

-       Use a piece of tissue to clean the length of it and remove grease or grime.

-       Get the lubricant for the machine from Cricut or a Cricut dealer.

-       Move the little carriage to the middle of the carriage barn.

-       Using a cotton puff, some of the lubricant onto the tip of the cotton puff.

-       You will need to swab a light coating of the lubricant on both sides of the carriage.

-       Once you have applied the lubricant, gently move the carriage from side to side.

-       Wipe off any excess lubricant with tissue paper.

Parts, Spares, and Services

Find your nearest Cricut supplier or dealer to learn about any maintenance or repair that may have to be done on the machine. If your device is still under warranty, it is best to get service from your local dealer instead of trying to tinker with it yourself.

Cricut offers parts and spares for nearly all of its current and older machines. These can be conveniently purchased online at their craft shop or your local Cricut dealer.

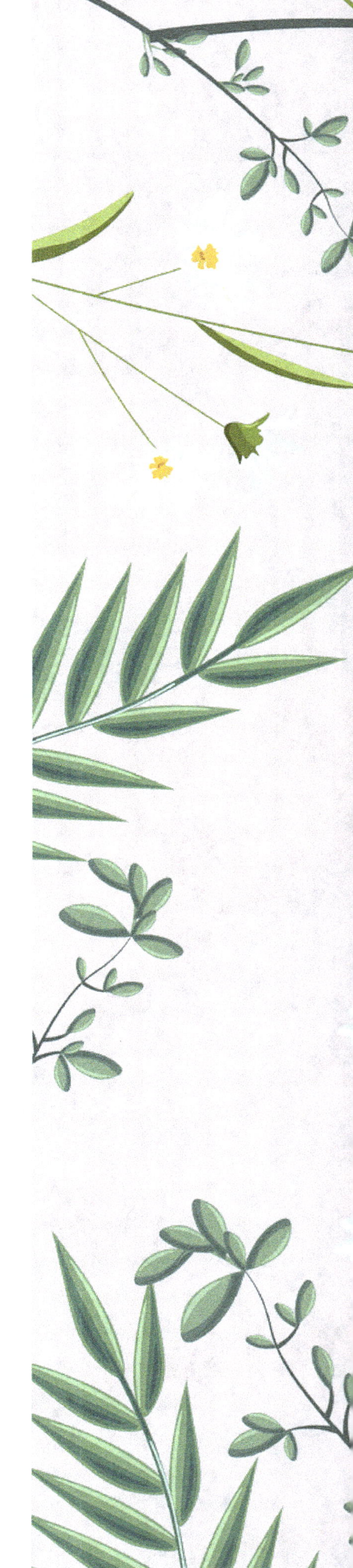

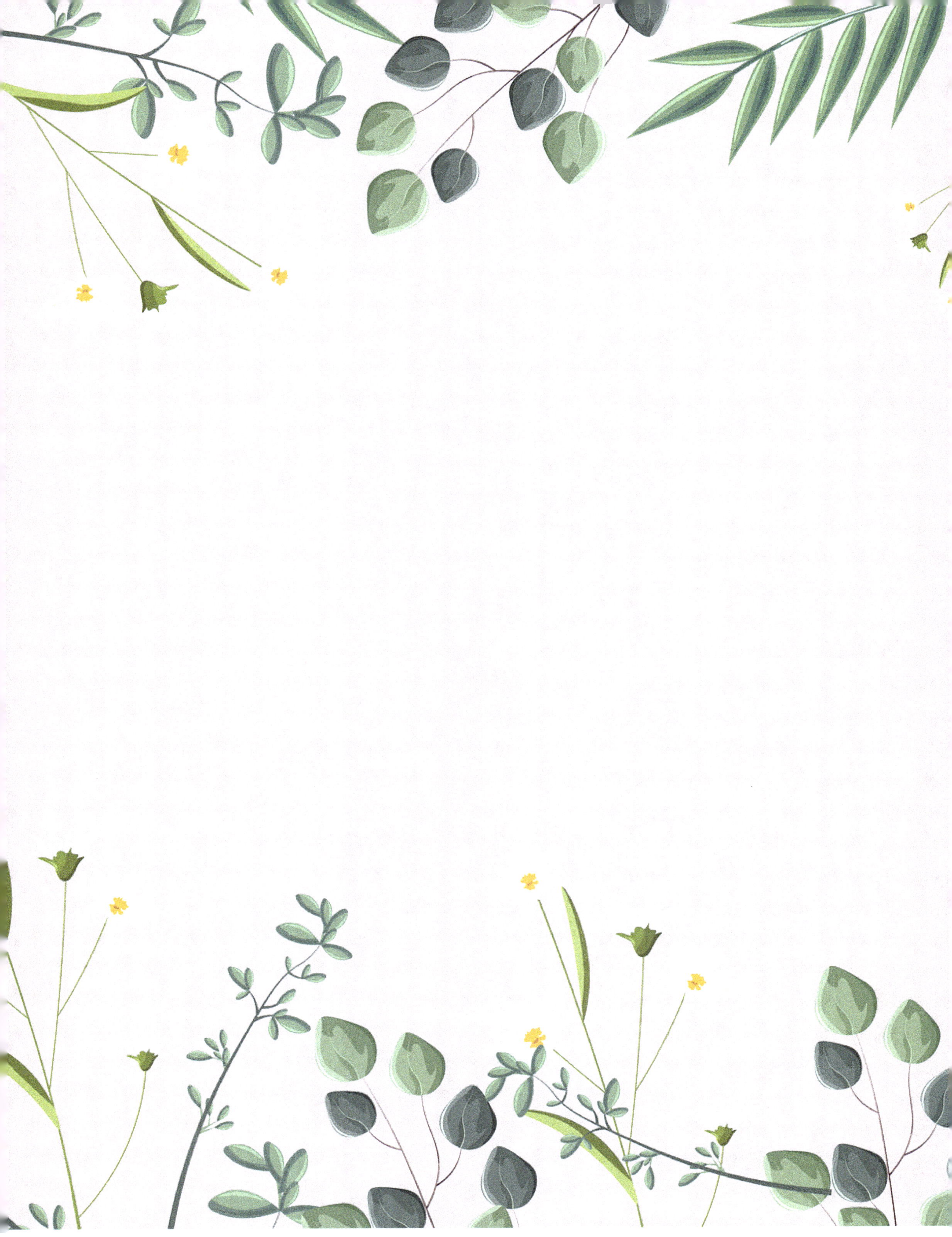

Conclusion

This may be the end of the "CRICUT EXPLORE AIR 2" book, but it is just the beginning of your crafting journey. Once you have gained the confidence to start trying out your designs, you will be amazed at what you can make with the Explore Air 2.

Don't fall into the trap of thinking you have to get all the accessories at once, either. The basics are fine, to begin with. Although it is very tempting to buy them all at once, it is more important to spend a bit extra on the different materials. The Cricut Explore Air 2 has hundreds of other materials to choose from.

As you design and get a feel for the different cut depths, blades, mats, and for navigating Design Space, you can slowly add to your accessories. Essential items to have in your kit are:
- A Weeding tool
- A Scraper or Brayer tool
- A pair of Tweezers
- At least the StandardGrip and LightGrip machine mats
- Some Cricut Pens
- The EasyPress Mat

With the above tools, you will be able to get a lot done. The EasyPress mat is included in the list because it works well with irons, too. The EasyPress mat is also very versatile for heat transfers. For items like T-shirts, canvas bags, etc., you can put the mat in the middle of the material to better transfer quality. It also makes the garment a lot easier to work with.

The Weeding tool is an essential item, as it gets into the tiniest of crevices to remove unwanted material. Used with the Tweezer, it can prolong the lives of your machine mats by getting stubborn material off of them.

To prolong the lives of items like your machine mats, you should keep the protective plastic covers that come with them. Before storing them, make sure you clean them and then pop the plastic back on them. You can run the machine mats under cold water to loosen stubborn items sticking them. If you do give them a rinse, stand them upright on a draining rack to dry afterward.

There is a host of information on the Cricut website that can improve your cutting skills.

Practice makes perfect. Use the projects listed in this book to help you improve upon your techniques. Use them as templates to add to, redesign, or create your unique designs.

Keep those crafting ideas going and remember the reason most people do arts and crafts is for enjoyment. With that being said, enjoy your new Cricut Explore Air 2, and keep crafting!

Thank
you !!